uaum's Quick Guide
to the Verbal SAT®

Other books in Schaum's Quick Guide Series

Schaum's Quick Guide to Writing Great Short Stories
Schaum's Quick Guide to Writing Great Essays
Schaum's Quick Guide to Writing Great Research Papers
Schaum's Quick Guide to Great Presentation Skills
Schaum's Quick Guide to Great Business Writing
Schaum's Quick Guide to Business Formulas

Schaum's Quick Guide to the Verbal SAT®

How to Add 100 Points or More to Your Score

Dawn B. Sova, Ph. D.

McGraw-Hill

New York   San Francisco   Washington, D.C.   Auckland   Bogotá
Caracas   Lisbon   London   Madrid   Mexico City   Milan
Montreal   New Delhi   San Juan   Singapore
Sydney   Tokyo   Toronto

Library of Congress Cataloging-in Publication Data

Sova, Dawn B.
  Schaum's quick guide to the verbal SAT® / Dawn Sova.
    p.   cm. — (Schaum's quick guide series)
  Includes index.
  ISBN 0-07-135401-8
  1. Scholastic Aptitude Test—Study guides. 2. English Language—Examinations—Study guides. 3. Universities and colleges—United States—Entrance examinations—Study guides.
  I. Title. II. Series.
  LB2353.57 .S68   2001
  378.1'662—dc21   00-033237

McGraw-Hill

*A Division of The **McGraw·Hill** Companies*

Copyright © 2001 by The McGraw-Hill Companies, Inc. All rights reserved. Printed in the United States of America. Except as permitted under the United States Copyright Act of 1976, no part of this publication may be reproduced or distributed in any form or by any means, or stored in a database or retrieval system, without the prior written permission of the publisher.

    2 3 4 5 6 7 8 9 0   DOC/DOC   0 6 5 4 3 2 1 0

ISBN 0-07-135401-8

The sponsoring editor for this book was Barbara Gilson, the editing supervisor was Ruth W. Mannino, and the production supervisor was Elizabeth Strange. It was set in Palatino by Inkwell Publishing Services.

Printed and bound by R. R. Donnelley and Sons Company.

SAT® is registered trademark of Educational Testing Service, Princeton, New Jersey, which does not endorse this book.

This publication is designed to provide accurate and authoritative information in regard to the subject matter covered. It is sold with the understanding that neither the author nor the publisher is engaged in rendering legal, accounting, or other professional service. If legal advice or other expert assistance is required, the services of a competent professional person should be sought.

—From a Declaration of Principles jointly adopted by a Committee of the American Bar Association and a Committee of Publishers

---

McGraw-Hill books are available at special quantity discounts to use as premiums and sales promotions, or for use in corporate training programs. For more information, please write to the Director of Special Sales, McGraw-Hill, Two Penn Plaza, New York, NY 10121-2298. Or contact your local bookstore.

 This book is printed on recycled, acid-free paper containing a minimum of 50 percent recycled de-inked fiber.

Contents

Preface	ix
Chapter 1: Building Your Vocabulary	1
Chapter 2: Sentence Completion	7
General Strategies for Sentence Completion Items	8
Using the Whole Sentence	8
Completing the Pair	9
Explaining Directly	10
Comparing	11
Comparing in a Negative Manner (Contrasting)	11
Identifying Word Sequences	13
Using Function Words	14
Chapter 3: Sentence Completion	17
Separating Connotation from Denotation	17
Separating Synonyms	19
Finding Words That Associate	20
Speaking Figuratively	21
Using Allusions	22
Finding Familiar Words	23
Chapter 4: Sentence Completion	25
Foreign Word Source	27

v

Chapter 5: Sentence Completions — 31
- Unmasking Impostor Words — 32
- Impostor Words Checkup Quiz — 32
- Sound-Alike Words—Homonyms — 32
- Homonyms Checkup Quiz — 36
- Look-Alike Words—Homographs — 36
- Homographs Checkup Quiz — 37

Chapter 6: Analogies — 39
- What Do Analogy Items Require? — 39
- Approaching Analogy Questions — 40
- General Analogies Quiz — 43

Chapter 7: Analogies — 51
- When You Don't Know the Parts of Speech — 52
- When You Don't Know the Main Word Pair Meanings — 53

Chapter 8: Analogy Types — 57
- Relating Size — 57
- Relating Units of Measurement — 58
- Relating Degrees of Intensity — 60

Chapter 9: Analogy Types — 63
- Relating Objects and Ideas to Specific Qualities or Conditions — 63
- Relating Objects or Ideas to Other Objects or Ideas — 65
- Relating Actions and Objects — 67
- Gender, Group, and Parent-Offspring Classification — 68

Chapter 10: Analogy Types — 71
- Relating the Whole to the Part — 71
- Relating the Container to Something Contained — 73
- Relating a General Term to a More Specific Term — 75

Chapter 11: Analogies — 77
- Relating People and Their Qualities — 77
- Relating People and Their Purposes — 79
- Relating People (or Subjects) to Places — 80

Chapter 12: Reading Comprehension — 83
- Developing Your Strategies — 83
- Reading and Understanding the Questions — 84
- Reading the Passages Effectively — 87
- Determining the Main Idea of the Passage — 88
- Single Passage or Dual (Paired) Passages? — 90

Chapter 13: Reading Passages — 93
- Strategies and Trigger Words for Finding Text Details — 93
- Finding Combined Details — 97

Chapter 14: Reading Passages — 101
- Developing Your Strategies — 101
- Making the Reasonable Choice — 103

Chapter 15: Reading Passages — 111
- Determining the Author's Purpose — 112
- Determining the Author's Attitude — 114
- Determining the Author's Tone — 116

Chapter 16: Reading Passages — 119
- Identifying Diction and Figurative Language — 119
- Terms That Evaluate Degree and Exclude — 122

Chapter 17: Practice Test 1 — 125

Chapter 18: Practice Test 1 Answers — 133
- Reading Comprehension (Questions 20-30) — 135

Chapter 19: Practice Test II	137
Chapter 20: Practice Test II Answers	147
Sentence Completions (Questions 1-15)	147
Reading Comprehension (Questions 16-30)	148
Chapter 21: Practice Test III	151
Chapter 22: Practice Test III Answers	159
Sentence Completions (Questions 1-12)	159
Analogies (Questions 13-22)	160
Reading Comprehension (Questions 23-30)	161
Index	163

Preface

Another SAT preparation book? Aren't the bookstore shelves already overflowing with guides that claim to contain the "hidden secrets" of the test and promise "instant success"?

The answer is an obvious yes. These books often dazzle readers with their promises of tricks and tips guaranteed to "beat the test," and they purport to offer actual or practice tests that simulate the difficulty levels of the SAT. Students take the tests, check their answers, and read the explanations. As a result, they may understand what they did right or wrong for a given item, but they *do not* learn how to approach test items that differ from those in the practice tests. Existing guides also don't teach students how to develop the basic verbal reasoning skills that will enable them to successfully respond to all three types of verbal questions on the test: *reading comprehension* (understanding and analyzing information in reading passages), *sentence completion* (recognizing relationships between parts of a sentence), and *analogies* (establishing relationships between pairs of words).

Schaum's Quick Guide to the Verbal SAT® is different. Instead of bombarding you with lengthy tests and canned responses, this book focuses on helping you to develop skills that you can apply to all types of verbal reasoning questions on the test. After mastering the basic verbal reasoning skills, you will confidently apply these new skills to even the most challenging SAT questions.

Dawn Sova

Schaum's Quick Guide to the Verbal SAT®

Chapter 1

Building Your Vocabulary

Can You Match the Pieces?

You have probably heard from many people that the way to earn a high score on the SAT is to learn thousands of new words. If you *really learned* them, the words would help a lot—but how many do you think most students learn when they try to cram thousands of words with definitions into their already overloaded brains? Very few.

Fortunately, you have a better way. Instead of learning specific words, you will have a lot more success if you learn the parts that make up the words—the prefixes, roots, and suffixes. You might even have some fun combining the parts and coming up with definitions for words that you never before knew!

Try this. The root "psych" means "mind" and the suffix "-ology" means "study of"; thus "psychology" means "study of the mind." Now, let's keep "psych" and add the root "iatr" meaning "healing" and the suffix "-ist" meaning "one who." We now have "psychiatrist," "one who heals the mind."

Words in English often combine prefixes, roots, and suffixes from Latin, Greek, and Anglo-Saxon to create meaning, so don't worry about identifying the origin. It's more important that you can identify the meaning. Review the list in Table 1-1 of some of the most common prefixes, roots, and suffixes.

Are you ready to create some words? Or to estimate the meanings of "SAT" words that you have placed on a personal "to-learn" list?

Why not combine a prefix with a root, or attach a suffix to another root? You might even combine two roots, connect two suffixes to a root, or pick your own combination.

bene + dictus + ion = benediction = a blessing

factus + ory = factory = a place where one makes or does

Table 1-1 List of Word Parts

Prefix	Meaning	Root	Meaning	Suffix	Meaning
ad-	toward	bene, bon, bonus	good, well	-ab, -al, -an, -ar, -ic, ical, -ine	like, related to
ambi-	both	dico, dictus	to say or tell	-able, -ible	able to
com-	with, together	facio, factus	to make or to do	-ance, -ence, -hood	state or quality of
contra-	against, opposite	fides	faith	-ar, -eer, -er, -or	one who, that which
				-arium, -ary, -erie, -ery, -ory	place where
dis-	apart from	iatr	healing	-ate, -iac	make, act, one who
e-, ex-	out	levis	light	-en	make
im-, in-	not	mar	sea	-et, -ette	little, small
pre-	before	naut, nav	ship, sail	-ical, -ine	related to, relating to
re-	back, again	plac	to please, appease, soothe	-ion, -ity	state, quality, act
				-ible	capable of
retro-	back, backward	phone	sound	-ist	one who
sub-	under	psych	mind	-ize	to make, to act
super-	above, beyond	rid, ris	laugh	-ly, -ous	having quality of
trans-	across	simulo	to copy	-ology	study of
ultra-	beyond, extremely	somn	sleep	-ship, -ty, -ure	state of, quality of, that which
vice-	in place of	techn	art or skill	-tude	state, quality of, act of
		urb	city	-ward, -wards	in the direction of
		volo	to wish, to be willing	-wise	in the manner of

levis + ity = levity = quality of being light
volo + eer = volunteer = one who is willing
sub + mar + ine = submarine = related to under the sea
ris + ible = risible = capable of laughing; able to excite laughter
urb + an = urban = related to city
techn + ical = technical = related to art or skill
simulo + tude = similitude = state of being a copy
sub + urb + an = suburban = related to under (or less than the city
naut + ical = nautical = related to ships
phone + ic = phonic = related to sound
in + somn + iac = insomniac = one who does not sleep
dis + simulo + ar = dissimilar = that which is not a copy
urb + an + ize = urbanize = to make like the city

Now, use the list of word parts in Table 1-1 as your clues to determine the meanings in the exercise.

Exercises

Example 1-1
  benevolent → _____

Example 1-2
  complacence → _____

Example 1-3
  contradict→ _____

Example 1-4
  fidelity→ _____

Example 1-5
  implacable→_____

Example 1-6
  levitate→ _____

Example 1-7
  naval→ _____

Example 1-8
    placater→ _____

Example 1-9
    predict→ _____

Example 1-10
    simulate→ _____

How close are your answers? We'll check these examples together, but you should use a dictionary when you practice this approach to word meanings in the future. Remember to analyze the parts carefully and attempt to come as close to the basic meanings of each part as you can.

THE ANSWERS (WELL, APPROXIMATELY)

Example 1-1
    benevolent = bene + volo + -ent = the state or quality of willing to be good

Example 1-2
    complacence = com- + plac + -ence = with the state of pleasure or appeasement

Example 1-3
    contradict = contra- + dictus = to say or to tell the opposite

Example 1-4
    fidelity = fides + -ity = an act or quality of faith

Example 1-5
    implacable = im- + plac + -able = not able to be soothed

Example 1-6
    levitate = levis + -ate = the act of making light

Example1- 7
    naval = nav + -al = related to ships

Example 1-8
    placater = plac + -ate + -er = one who acts to soothe or appease

Example 1-9
    predict = pre- + dictus = to speak before or in advance

Example 1-10

simulate = simulo + -ate = the act of copying

Check these approximations against a dictionary and you'll see that using the word parts to determine meaning on the SAT Verbal Reasoning section will bring you closer than you might realize.

Now give yourself a hand—and let's move on!

Chapter 2

Sentence Completion

What's the Context?

The sentence-completion items of the SAT verbal sections test both your knowledge of vocabulary and your reasoning ability. Whether you are asked to complete one blank or two blanks in a sentence, understanding how context can be an effective aid in making the right choice is an important step in making the right word choice.

How many words that you use daily did you actually learn by looking up in a dictionary? Not as many as you think, because we learn most words through experience in a specific situation that supplies the context to understand them. Sharpening your skills in identifying the meanings of words from their context is not only valuable in mastering the sentence completion section of the SAT. The reading comprehension passages will be much easier to understand, as well, if you know word meanings.

Even if you don't know the meaning of sentence-completion choices, you will usually be able to make a fairly good guess if you pay close attention to how the blank relates to the rest of the words in the sentence. Once you have an idea of the type of word needed, you will then use your skill with word parts, sharpened in Chapter 1, to determine the meanings of the unfamiliar word choices. In this chapter you will learn to use your reasoning ability to identify how the words of the sentence provide a context, through pairings of words, direct explanation, comparison, contrast, sequences, or inclusion of function words. You will also learn which types of contexts may be found in one-blank or two-blank sentence-completion items.

General Strategies for Sentence Completion Items

In this and the following three chapters, you will learn to use context, word clues, foreign words, and trick words to your advantage in filling the blanks in sentence-completion items. Remember that the directions on the test ask you to select the word that best completes each blank, and so you will have to use a variety of strategies in approaching sentence-completion items.

Before you work on such individual skills, learn the five general sentence-completion strategies:

1. Try out each choice in the blank before making your final choice, and use the process of elimination to remove irrelevant and incorrect choices.
2. Fill the blank with a word of your own before making your choices. Then select the choice that best matches your word.
3. Identify key words in the sentence, and determine if they indicate that a contrast, a result, or support is needed.
4. Try out the first word of pair choices in sentence-completion items having two blanks; eliminate the choices in which the first word does not make sense in the sentence.
5. Try out both words of only those pair choices in which the first word matches sentence-completion items having two blanks.

Using the Whole Sentence

The entire sentence may function as a context clue in helping you to correctly fill the blank in a sentence-completion item, once you are comfortably sure of what the word choices mean. Rather than look for a match immediately, ignore the choices and attempt to substitute your own word for the blank. Then review the answer choices and find the choice that best matches your word. When you are confronted by unfamiliar words, use your skills in matching prefixes, roots, and suffixes to determine meaning.

One-Blank Example

Members of the _____ family could not escape notice when they ventured out in public during their vacation.

    (A) wealthy (B) arrogant (C) prominent
    (D) indolent (E) visiting

Approach: The expression "could not escape notice" suggests that the family is well known and routinely draws attention wherever it goes. After making this observation, you can immediately eliminate the negative (B) and (D). You can also eliminate the neutral (E) as well. This leaves a choice between (A) and (C). "Wealthy" families *may* be well known, but they are *not necessarily* well known. This leaves (C) "prominent," as the best choice.

Two-Blank Example

The _____ political candidate will not give up, and she _____ her followers to increase their efforts.

        (A) foolish .. forbids
        (B) exhausted .. encourages
        (C) defeated .. reminds
        (D) tenacious .. exhorts
        (E) novice .. orders

Approach: Try out the pairs of choices to determine which provides the perfect fit for the sentence. Beginning with (A), if you insert "foolish" in the first blank, you run into difficulty in trying to make "forbids" logically complete the meaning of the sentence. A candidate may be "foolish" for not giving up, but if she were not giving up, she would not forbid her followers to increase their efforts. On the contrary, she would encourage them to do so. If you try choice (B), you find that you have a barely possible answer in which an "exhausted" candidate "encourages" a continuation of the campaign. In choice (C), the word "defeated" contradicts the statement "will not give up," because someone defeated cannot go on, so this choice is eliminated. Choice (D) describes the candidate as "tenacious," or not one to give up, which is a very good possible answer. Trying out the second word of the pair, you find that a candidate such as that described in the first part of the sentence would logically "exhort," make an urgent appeal to, her followers to increase their efforts. Despite finding an apparently good fit, try choice (E). The paired terms do not provide as clear and necessary a relationship as those in (D) and offer only a barely possible answer.

Completing the Pair

A sentence that contains either repeated ideas or words may provide the correct meaning of the word needed to fill in the blank. When a sentence contains such pairing, knowing one of the words or ideas can make your choice easier.

Example

The road to success is paved with hard work and _____.

  (A) compromise (B) elegance (C) happiness
    (D) diligence (E) laziness

Approach: In this sentence, the phrase "hard work" is paired with the word required by the blank. Try out each of the word choices and see how well each matches the phrase. Use the process of elimination to remove (B), (C), and (E) from consideration, because "elegance" and "happiness" are not terms that usually describe or are associated with "hard work," and "laziness" is in direct opposition to the term. That leaves choices (A) and (D). "Compromise" *might* be a choice, because it means "to see other sides" or "to make an adjustment in point of view," but it is not as good a choice as (D), "diligence," which means "persistent application to one's work."

Explaining Directly

Sentences containing this type of context clue actually provide an explanation of the word required by the blank. Such explanations of the meaning of the needed word may appear in the form of subordinate clauses or participial phrases, an appositive (a word or phrase set off by a comma, dash, or pair of commas), or a phrase beginning with the conjunction "for" or "because."

Example

Sherri's _____ entry in the essay-writing contest, arriving two weeks after the deadline for entries, was not accepted by the judges.

  (A) articulate (B) dilatory (C) hand-written
    (D) prompt (E) controversial

Approach: In the sentence, the participial phrase "arriving two weeks after the deadline for entries" describes the nature of the entry, which the phrase indicates as late. Thus, the blank requires a negative descriptive term to complete the meaning of the sentence, and so you can eliminate (A) and (D), which are favorable terms. You can also eliminate choice (C), because a "hand-written" entry is neither favorable nor unfavorable. This leaves the unfavorable associations of choices (B) and (E). You might not know the meaning of the word "dilatory," but knowing that "controversial" means "subject to dispute or disagreement," you can also eliminate choice (E). This leaves "dilatory," which means "tending or meant to delay."

Comparing

Sentences with either "as" or "like" usually contain comparisons that suggest meanings for the word required by the blank. Before attempting to fit one of the word choices into the blank, review the compared word or meaning and come up with a word of your own. You can then match your word to the choices.

Example

His _____ way of introducing the celebrities was as elaborate as the rhinestone-encrusted costume that he wore on the show.

(A) understated   (B) well-known   (C) flamboyant
(D) eccentric   (E) indecisive

Approach: The comparison clearly suggests that the person's way of introducing celebrities is showy and noticeable, "as elaborate as the rhinestone-encrusted costume." Thus, (A) and (E) can be eliminated, because they contrast with "elaborate." "Well-known" is not suggested by the sentence, and so (B) is eliminated. You might consider (D) as a possibility, but being "eccentric" does not necessarily mean being noticeable. This leaves choice (C), "flamboyant," which matches very well with the concept of being showy and noticeable.

Comparing in a Negative Manner (Contrasting)

Sentence-completion items often contain negative comparisons, statements that provide clues to meaning by telling what the word needed in the blank is *not*. Such contrasts may be signaled by the inclusion of any one of the following terms within the sentence: "but," "not," "either-or," "neither-nor," "although," "though," "never," "instead."

One-Blank Example

City dwellers often long for the peaceful harmony of farm life, although they find the loud _____ of urban life difficult to leave behind.

    (A) happiness   (B) dirtiness   (C) friendliness
           (D) cacophony   (E) streets

Approach: The contrast term "although" controls the choice of answer in this sentence. The blank is contrasted with "harmony," as "peaceful" contrasts with "noisy," and the word choice for the blank must be unfavorable. For one reason or another, choices (A), (B), (C), and (E) are faulty choices. "Happiness" and "friendliness" are favorable and do not contrast with "harmony." "Dirtiness" is unfavorable, but it is not parallel with "harmony," while "streets" is neutral. Thus, (D), "cacophony," is the only term that provides the needed contrast to "harmony."

Two-Blank Example

Aaron did not allow his father's _____ behavior to influence his future; instead, this generous man became known for his _____ toward others.

           (A) unfriendly .. hatred
           (B) parsimonious .. largesse
           (C) noncommittal .. anger
           (D) benevolent .. stinginess
           (E) arrogant .. indifference

Approach: The contrast suggested by "instead" is the key to determining the correct word pair choice. In this sentence, the contrast is between negative behavior and positive, specifically generous, behavior because Aaron is a "generous man" in contrast to his father. Therefore, the first blank must contain an unfavorable descriptive term. If you try choice (A), the first term is unfavorable, but the "generous man" of the second part of the sentence would not show "hatred" toward others. Choice (B) sounds good, because it creates a contrast between the "parsimonious behavior" and the "generous man," and the "largesse" matches the sense of the "generous man." Although this seems to be a good choice, we have to try our other options. Choice (C) provides a neutral first term, and the word "anger" contradicts the behavior of the "generous man," and it doesn't work. Neither does choice (D), where the first term, "benevolent," would not fit someone who was ungenerous, the father; nor does "stinginess" describe a "generous man." The first term of choice (E) might apply, but the "generous man" is contradicted by the term "indifference." Thus, choice (B) remains the best choice.

Identifying Word Sequences

The way in which words are arranged in a sentence may often provide clues to the meaning of the blank. When arranged in a sequence, words will show an increase in intensity, and knowing just one of the words will help you to figure out those remaining. When two blanks must be completed, such words as "first" and "then" are often used, and the second alternative is usually an outgrowth of the first.

One-Blank Example

By midday, the steady pressure of the pack on his back was painful, and by nightfall the continued pressure had become _____.

      (A) enjoyable (B) repeated (C) pleasant
      (D) excruciating (E) noticeable

Approach: The sequence of words begins with the pressure being "painful" in midday, and the change occurs over time and it is next described at nightfall. The use of the conjunction "and" indicates that the pressure has increased in intensity, creating the need for the choice of a word having an unfavorable connotation, so (A) and (C) are eliminated. Choice (B) is noncommittal and contributes nothing to the sentence, and neither does (E). Only choice (D) indicates an increase in the intensity of the pain due to the pressure of the pack.

Two-Blank Example

The development of events was inspiring, beginning with the _____ of the neighborhood and ending with the _____ of the people's pride.

      (A) demolition .. obliteration
      (B) revitalization .. restoration
      (C) education .. announcement
      (D) memory .. destruction
      (E) adaptation .. insulting

Approach: The sequence in the sentence is established with the words "beginning with" and "ending with" and suggests that the second alternative is an outgrowth of the first. When you test the choices, you must keep this sequence in mind and be certain that the order of the words that fill the blanks maintains this sequence. You must also keep in mind that the choices must also fulfill the demand stated in the opening clause, that "the development of events was inspiring." Given this requirement, choices (A), (D), and (E) are unacceptable, because the sequence is unclear and, more important, the "obliteration," "destruction," and "insulting" of the pride of the people would not be "inspiring." In choice C, the "education" of a neighborhood would not necessarily result in an "announcement" of people's pride. However, choice (B) does work because the "revitalization" of a neighborhood would be followed by the "restoration" of pride.

Using Function Words

In many sentences, function words such as prepositions and conjunctions are vital to show connections and relationships between the major content words (nouns, verbs, adjectives, adverbs) that give basic meaning. Function words may change or redirect the basic meanings of the content words, and they may even intensify their meanings. Do not be surprised if the entire meaning of a sentence depends solely on one, seemingly insignificant, function word. To make more effective word choices in sentence-completion items that contain function words, memorize the lists below to learn the great effect that each function word has upon a sentence.

Following are some of the many function words that you will encounter:

Negative: neither, no, no one, nobody, not

Opposite direction: although, but, however, nevertheless, otherwise, unless

Same direction: and, also, as well, besides

Degree: somewhat, too, very

Time: after, before, during, meanwhile, then, till, until, when, while

Cause and effect: as, because, for, it, since, so that, yet

Numbers: few, less, many, more, some, one

Example

Before the children ran through the door with their muddy and wet boots, the freshly waxed kitchen floor was _____.

(A) grimy (B) immaculate (C) affluent
(D) disheveled (E) diminished

Approach: The sentence begins with the function word "before," which provides a time frame for the "freshly waxed kitchen floor" preceding the entrance of the children "with muddy and wet boots." The change that their entrance suggests is unfavorable, and so the word choice that you seek must be the opposite, or favorable. Reviewing the choices, you can eliminate (A), because the floor will become grimy after the children run through. Choices (C) and (E) have no logical connection to the sentence; you can also eliminate (D), because people, and not floors, become "disheveled." Thus, (B) is the answer.

Observing the context of words in a sentence often provides you with a clear path to the correct answer. If it does not, you may want to solve the mystery of word choice by using the clues that appear in Chapter 3.

Chapter 3
Sentence Completion

Have You a Clue?

Words within a sentence and the signals of the word choices often provide hints that lead you to the right word choice in answering sentence-completion items. You just have to train yourself to recognize where the signs are pointing and follow their direction. Among such signs that direct you in making word choices are understanding how the connotation of a word differs from its denotation, identifying how words that are synonyms may have important shades of difference, knowing how related words associate, applying the literary techniques of figurative language and allusions, and finding familiar words among the seemingly unfamiliar.

Separating Connotation from Denotation

Most of us are on safe ground when we deal with the denotative meanings of words, because we can point to a dictionary definition and most dictionaries will agree closely in defining a word. The problems in communication—and especially in completing items on the SAT verbal sections—arise when the suggested meanings, the *connotations*, of words are the issue. Connotations of words are the range of associations that surround them and that define more specifically than the dictionary meaning.

You will probably not have much of a problem when the issue is a simple matter of deciding if words have favorable or unfavorable associations, i.e., "competitors" as opposed to "rivals." The trouble actually arises when the sentence asks you to look more deeply into the meaning and to combine the context skills that you reviewed in Chapter 2 with your knowledge of the connotations of a word or of several words to make the correct choice.

One-Blank Example

In her effort to win the role of a young teenager, the 30-year-old actress starved herself, which left her looking _____ rather than youthfully slender.

(A) thin (B) fit (C) trim (D) underfed (E) emaciated

Approach: Each of the five choices offers some aspect of the result of weight loss, but the sentence sends a clear message that a negative term is needed to fill the blank. The necessarily unfavorable tone would not be supplied by "fit" or "trim," and so you can eliminate choices (B) and (C). You can also eliminate "thin" and "underfed," choices (A) and (D), because they are too neutral to supply the negative tone implied by the word "starved" in the sentence. This leaves you with choice (E) to convey the association of extreme, debilitating thinness.

Two-Blank Example

The students began each day by respectfully _____ the new teacher, who _____ arranged the items and papers on her desk.

(A) copying .. carelessly
(B) mocking .. meticulously
(C) parodying .. slowly
(D) imitating .. carefully
(E) honoring .. angrily

Approach: After examining the sentence, you will recognize that the word "respectfully" determines that the type of word needed in the first blank must have a *favorable* connotation. You can immediately eliminate choices (B) and (C), because they are negative in meaning. If you now look at the second word in each of the remaining pair choices (A), (D), and (E), you find that "carelessly" in choice (A) and "angrily" in choice (E) are not consistent with the favorable connotation required by the sentence. You are, thus, left with choice (D). Substitute the possible answers to see if they fit the sentence.

The students began each day by respectfully *imitating* the new teacher, who *carefully* arranged the items and papers on her desk.

Sentences of this type require that you use what you learned in Chapter 2 to identify meanings of unfamiliar words and then find the difference between similar words by determining their connotations.

Separating Synonyms

Synonyms pose a special problem when you are asked to make the *best* word choice in a sentence-completion, analogy, and even a reading comprehension item. We often use words of similar meaning interchangeably in everyday conversation, and this habit spells disaster (as in low verbal scores) when carried on to testing. You should begin immediately to practice word discrimination—and use the most specific words possible when you speak. Do not be surprised if at least two benefits result—(1) people will more fully understand your meaning, and (2) your verbal scores will soar.

Let's look at an example from our lives, before venturing into SAT examples. When you are prevented from doing what you wish, do you feel "peeved," "displeased," "angry," "discontent," or "irate"? These varying degrees of emotion are all possible reactions—and synonyms—but your *specific* reaction depends upon what the activity is and how important it is to you. Given one set of circumstances, you might describe yourself as merely "peeved" or "displeased," while another situation might make you "irate." The same range of differences applies to selecting among synonyms to complete sentences. Not only do you have to determine the context for the word needed, but you must consider the connotations of the choices, as well.

One-Blank Example

The author William Sidney Porter preferred to publish stories under the _____ of O. Henry.

(A) alias   (B) name   (C) pseudonym
(D) title   (E) appellation

Approach: Answer (C) is correct because a writer uses a "pseudonym." Although the other word choices also refer to names, choices (B) and (E) are too general, and choice (D) refers to a specific position. Choice (A) does mean a name other than one's own, but "alias" also carries a negative association that is generally applied.

Two-Blank Example

The political candidates have _____ each other as enemies of the common people who would _____ tax breaks to the rich.

(A) labeled .. deny

(B) branded .. provide

(C) named .. prevent

(D) called .. revoke

(E) complimented .. give

Approach: The two-blank items require you to use multiple skills in selecting the correct pair of words to complete the sentence. The answers include two similar sets of words, "labeled" and "branded," "named" and "called," plus the word "complimented." Because the first words of the remaining word pairs are similar, you will have to examine the second word in each of the remaining pairs. You can immediately eliminate choice (E), because "enemies of the common people" is not a compliment to a politician for whom votes mean winning. If you try choices (A), (C), and (D), you find that the sentence contradicts itself when they are inserted. Only choice (B) fits perfectly to convey the negative name-calling and the reason for which a politician might be "branded" with such a charge.

Finding Words That Associate

We often view words as related to each other because of the way we learned them. The connections or associations may be due to the area of language from which they are drawn, such as "walk," "strut," "gambol," and "stroll." Or they may depend upon their use in performing certain tasks, such as "pen," "ink," "pencil," and "typewriter." Sentence-completion items on the SAT that ask you to associate words are often the easiest to answer. Even if you may not know the *specific* meaning of a word, you can probably eliminate all incorrect word choices as long as you have some idea that a word is related to the cluster of words that appear in the sentence.

Example

The angry, glowering appearance of the clouds suggested that the trip home would be _____ by difficulties.

(A) characterized (B) plagued (C) supported
(D) expedited (E) lightened

Approach: The combination of such terms as "angry," "glowering," and "difficulties" suggests that the answer must be associated in tone and meaning with these words. All three words emphasize the unfavorable weather conditions, and like them, the answer must also convey the sense of difficulty and duress. Choices (C), (D), and (E) contradict this meaning, because they are positive in tone and promise favorable results, while choice (A) is neutral. Only "plagued," choice (B), conveys the same unfavorable tone as the key words in the sentence.

Speaking Figuratively

Most of us create a strict separation between the terms that we apply to literature and those that we use in everyday writing to express ourselves. We are often surprised to learn just how often we use metaphors and similes to express ourselves in speech and in writing. The people who create the verbal items for the SAT are aware of this, however, and many vocabulary and reading comprehension questions rely on your ability to identify and to use figurative language.

Let's review two important terms.

Metaphor. A comparison between two apparently unlike entities that enriches our own expression with the associations that the comparison brings. We say that someone or something is someone or something else.

Example: The *woman* is a *tower of strength.*

Simile. A comparison between two apparently unlike entities that uses the word "like" or "as." We say that someone or something *is like* someone or something else. Because the comparison does not convey a complete transfer of all characteristics—only similarities—it is a less powerful comparison.

Example: He is *as clumsy as a puppy.*

In the *metaphor* example, the sentence states that the woman has all the characteristics of a tower of strength. In contrast, in the *simile* example, the sentence states that he is only similar to but not fully the same as a puppy.

Example

Listening to the audience, the singer felt his happiness _____ like an eagle in the sky.

    (A) inflate   (B) increase   (C) develop
           (D) shatter   (E) soar

Approach: The word choices offer different possibilities, all of which might logically relate to an individual's happiness while listening to audience reaction after a performance. The deciding factor in making the right word choice is the simile of the eagle, which does not (A) "inflate," (B) "increase," or (D) "shatter." Choice (C) is also incorrect because "develop" is a vague verb to apply to the majestic eagle, which does "soar," choice (E), through the sky.

Using Allusions

Selecting word choices that contain allusions can be easier if you have a fair knowledge of history, names, literature, or religion—but do not despair if this is not the case. You can still use all the context skills that are covered in Chapter 2 to achieve the same great results—spotting the allusions just simplifies the task.

What is an allusion? It is simply a word that contains a reference to a historical, religious, or literary figure, place, or incident. Most of us know that someone described as having "herculean" strength must be very strong—like the Greek demigod Hercules. To be "laconic" is to be a person of few words, an unexpressive person such as the Greek soldiers of Lakonia, the dominant city of which was Sparta.

You didn't know that? Don't worry. After so many years of history, literature, and other subjects in school, you have probably learned many allusions that you are not even aware of. And even if you overlook them, you can always use context skills to determine the answer.

Example

A new administrator who replaces a popular predecessor should take pains to gain the confidence of employees in order to avoid retaliation by _____ who resent his appointment.

    (A) subordinates   (B) zealots   (C) visitors
        (D) coworkers   (E) observers

Approach: Recognizing the term "zealots," which was the name of a radical political and religious Hebrew sect that openly resisted

Roman rule in ancient Palestine, makes choice (B) immediate. Even if you don't know the allusion, you can still determine the correct answer by using the process of elimination. "Visitors" and "observers," choices (C) and (E), may resent the new administrator, but the terms do not imply any negative actions or efforts to retaliate. "Subordinates" and "coworkers," choices (A) and (D), *might* or *might not* retaliate, but the terms themselves are neutral, and they contain no suggestion of open resistance. The term "zealots," however, in association with the strongly worded phrase "who resent his appointment," guides you through the process of elimination to select the correct choice (B).

Finding Familiar Words

Knowing the meanings of word parts (prefix, root, suffix) helps you to find meaning in longer words that may intimidate you at first. Short words seem to be so much easier to understand and to remember. To strengthen your ability to recognize familiar words that might be embedded within lengthy and unfamiliar words, learn the lists of word parts that appear in Chapter 1—and pay especial attention to the roots, which form the basis for even the lengthiest words. When you face a lengthy, unfamiliar word, you can easily determine its meaning by finding the shorter and more familiar root word within it.

Example

The new rules have been _____ in stopping the theft of widgets from the factory, because we continue to lose 1,000 units per month.

        (A) interesting   (B) excellent   (C) welcome
        (D) ineffectual   (E) useful

Approach: The key words in the sentence are "stopping" and "because," the second of which indicates that a result has been achieved. If the new rules *have* stopped the theft, then the result would *not* be to "continue to lose 1,000 units per month." Therefore, you must locate a word choice that indicates the failure to stop the theft. The root word of choice (D) is "effect," but the prefix "in-" indicates a failed rather than a successful effort to bring about an effect, so (D) is the correct choice. Choices (B), (C), and (E) are incorrect because "excellent," "welcome," and "useful" suggest the success of the rules. Choice (A), "interesting," is noncommittal and provides no indication of success. Thus, the only choice is (D).

Once again, when you use the above approach and still do not locate a root word, you can use the process of elimination and context skills to determine the answer.

We'll now move on from the mysteries of word clues to the intrigue of foreign words that are important elements of the English language.

Chapter 4
Sentence Completion

Do Foreign Words Count?

Knowing a language other than English can enrich your vocabulary and increase your knowledge of words both to help you to communicate more effectively *and* to increase your scores on the SAT verbal section. While you may be *most* familiar with words that have entered the English language from Italy, France, or Spain, you should also be aware of the numerous words that we now take for granted that had their origins in China, Africa, Germany, India, Persia, Russia, Poland, Syria, Morocco, and Mesopotamia (yes!).

Some words entered the English language whole and have remained so, that is, without any change to their spelling or pronunciation. Others, of necessity, have changed from their original forms, either because English does not have the symbols necessary to keep the original spelling and form or because the 26 letters of the English alphabet do not have sounds to represent the word in its original form.

The range of foreign borrowings is diverse, but certain types of terms are more common to one language source than to others, as Table 4-1 shows.

Table 4-1

Languages	Types of Words Contributed
African	Names for exotic animals, names of foods
American English	Technical terms and inventions
American Indian	Plants used for food
Arabic	Science and mathematics
Dutch	Seafaring and sea-related terms
French	Fashion, foods
German	Science and chemistry

Italian	Architecture and music
Persian	Fruits and flowers
Spanish	Objects in the American Old West

Table 4-2 lists some of the words that are now part of the English language, the definitions of which you will find in an English dictionary. How many of them do you know? The chance is that most are familiar to you. If any are not familiar, then look up their definitions in a dictionary. Learn as many of them as you can, and you will increase your chance of doing well in answering sentence completion, analogy, and reading comprehension questions.

Table 4-2

Language Source	Words Borrowed
African	bananas, chimpanzee, gnu, hominy, ibis, maize, pecan, succotash, squash, yam
American English	cellophane, e-mail, fax, thermos
American Indian	barbecue, potato
Arabic	alchemy, alcohol, algebra, algorithm, apricots, assassin, candy, caramel, chemistry, cipher, coffee, garble, hazard, nadir, sherbet, syrup, zenith, zero
Chinese	ketchup, kowtow, tea
Dutch	bulwark, deck, dock, freeboater, hoist, jib, skipper, sloop, Yankee
French	azimuth, bayonet, beret, boudoir, boulevard, cambric, chapeau, cop, coward, cravat, cretin, cretonne, croissant, curfew, debonair, denim, essay, fanfare, flamboyant, forest, march, mayonnaise, mistress, mound, omelet, parliament, pedigree, porcelain, regret, rich, right, soup, suede, target, tennis, turquoise, umpire, utopia, viand
German	bismuth, boat, camp, campus, champion, cobalt, cologne, dollar, Fahrenheit, frankfurter, freedom, gneiss, hamburger, husband, light, love, mark, night, old, quartz, queen, rucksack, shale, sleep, time, wedding, witness, work, world, zinc
Greek	abacus, allegory, barbarian, chaos, chasm, cheers, circus, demon, gorilla, heresy, idea, ideal, idol, laconic, nemesis, ostracize, planet, search, sugar, sycophant, thermostat, thesis, tyranny, wine

Hebrew	amen, bucolic, bulimia, cherub, cider, hallelujah, Jehovah, jubilee, pharisee, sabbath, seraph, shibboleth
Hindi	juggernaut, pundit
Hungarian	citron, coach
Indian	calico, catamaran, curry, ginger, pariah
Italian	addict, alarm, arcade, argosy, aria, balcony, ballot, cab, cantaloupe, carnival, chapel, colonnade, corridor, italic, jeans, malaria, opera, piano, portico, soprano
Japanese	karate
Malayan	amok, ketchup
Mesopotamian	muslin
Mexican	avocados, cocoa, tabasco, tomato
Moroccan	tangerine
Persian	bazaar, checkmate, jasmine, lemon, lilac, mogul, orange, peach, tulip
Polish	mazurka, polka
Portuguese	jaguar, mandarin
Russian	ukase
Scottish	cheviot, whisky
Spanish	adobe, alpaca, bizarre, bronco, canyon, charlatan, chocolate, companion, corral, lariat, lettuce, palaver, quinine, saffron, sherry, spaniel, title
Syrian	damask
Turkish	fez, turkey

After you review the words in Table 4-2, take the following quiz to test your knowledge of some of the many foreign words that have enriched our language. Do not look at the answers until after you have made your choices. You might be surprised at what you don't know!

Foreign Word Source

1. Someone who has run *amok* has been involved in a
    (A) marathon   (B) political contest   (C) fit of rage
    (D) business   (E) race of animals

2. An individual who is a *mogul* is a(n)
   (A) teller of lies   (B) surfer   (C) winner of awards
   (D) elderly person   (E) powerful person
3. To *hoist* a flag is to
   (A) lower it   (B) transport it   (C) raise it
   (D) fold it   (E) retire it from service
4. If designated a *pariah,* you would be a(n)
   (A) fish   (B) visionary   (C) religious leader
   (D) innovator   (E) outcast
5. The action of a *juggernaut* is to
   (A) perform technical tasks   (B) crush everything in its path
   (C) travel into space   (D) perform in a circus
   (E) hold a civil service job
6. The person who reaches the *nadir* of a career is at
   (A) the highest point   (B) a plateau   (C) the lowest point
   (D) the beginning   (E) the end
7. Listening to an *aria,* you will enjoy the sound of
   (A) a sermon   (B) a jazz song   (C) a tropical bird
   (D) a speech   (E) a melody in an opera
8. The character whose role in a play is that of a *sycophant* is a(n)
   (A) leading lady   (B) insincere flatterer   (C) sexy starlet
   (D) male lead   (E) murderer
9. A *charlatan* is someone who
   (A) makes unique pastries   (B) works at the racetrack
   (C) serves as an aide to a king   (D) pretends to be an expert
   (E) holds specialized but worthless knowledge
10. An *assassin* is specifically the following:
    (A) a murderer   (B) a terrorist
    (C) the killer of a politically important person
    (D) the killer of large numbers of people   (E) a religious fanatic

Now, check your answers against those below. How did you do?

ANSWERS

1. C   2. E   3. C   4. E   5. B   6. C   7. E   8. B   9. D   10. C

Review the word chart to locate other words that you might be unsure of and learn their meanings. You never know when they will appear in one of the SAT verbal sections.

We have one more chapter to cover before we leave sentence completions. In Chapter 5, you will identify words that are often confused, because of a variety of reasons. Some of the words have an identical source, but they have acquired different meanings over time, while others are often confused because they sound alike even though they have different functions or meanings. Many are new words that have been created by combining parts of old words in unique ways. Whatever your strengths, you will find this renewed familiarity with how the English language changes to be a valuable way of increasing your verbal skills.

Chapter 5

Sentence Completions

What's the Trick?

The English language is constantly changing—as new words are added, old words are phased out, and many words change in meaning. A good vocabulary no longer means simply memorizing lists containing thousands of words. Instead, you must pay attention to the changes of use that words undergo, and always remain open to the creations of new words and expressions required by new discoveries and processes.

Environmental concerns have added such phrases as "hazardous waste" and "acid rain," while space exploration has given us "launch window," "space shuttle," and "quark." The computer industry has had great impact on language, changing the meanings of such words as "monitor," "processor," and "computer" from nouns that described human beings who carried out such functions as "monitoring," "processing," and "computing" to nouns that name equipment. New words continue to enter the English language, and so no list created today could hope to remain complete for long. Your best means of remaining current and of increasing your vocabulary is to read extensively—newspapers, magazines, and any other type of nonfiction.

What you can improve by studying word lists is your mastery of frequently confused words, *impostor words* that are close enough in sound to seem to have one meaning but that actually mean something else, such as "elicit" and "illicit." Study *homophones*, words that are spelled identically but that have different definitions and, sometimes, different pronunciations. Master *homonyms*, words that sound alike but are spelled differently and have different definitions. Learn the spelling, sound, and definition of the range of confusing words so that you can easily determine context and select the correct answer—every time.

Unmasking Impostor Words

You know what impostor words are—they are the frequently misused words that are close enough in sound or spelling to another word to create confusion in their meanings and use. "Effect" often slips into slots meant for "affect," and writers mistakenly make "illusions" instead of "allusions." The difference of a few letters or a slight pronunciation variation fails to protect us from using one for the other, especially under pressure. And that is why we must deal with those impostor words now—because you will definitely be under pressure when you respond to the SAT verbal questions.

The only way to conquer the impostors is to memorize them. Examine the list in Table 5-1 and decide now that you will never again be fooled by an impostor.

Impostor Words Checkup Quiz

Underline the correct word in each sentence below *without* consulting the words in Table 5-1. Answers appear at the end of this chapter.

1. Employee (moral, morale) at the office was very low after the president announced that the company would lay off nearly 100 people.
2. After completing all the coursework for a degree in computer engineering, he will earn a much higher salary (than, then) a graduate of a liberal arts program.
3. Few noises bother (quiet, quite) as much as the sound of a fingernail scraping across a chalkboard.
4. Does anyone really know how this invention will (affect, effect) the current approach to heart surgery?
5. We expect that the United States will vote to (censor, censure) the President for his conduct unbecoming his office in the recent international incident.

Sound-Alike Words—Homonyms

The problem with homonyms, sometimes called "homophones," is that what you hear may not necessarily be the word that you must use to answer a sentence-completion, analogy, or reading comprehension question. Be especially careful in selecting your answer when sound-alike words are among the choices. Table 5-2 lists some commonly confused homonyms.

Table 5-1 Impostor Words

Word	Definition	Word	Definition
adapt	To change or fit to make something suitable	adopt	To take something and to make it one's own
affect	To influence, produce a change; the conscious subjective aspect of an emotion	effect	Anything brought about by a cause or change; to cause to come into being
bazaar	A market or street of shops	bizarre	Very odd in manner or appearance
censor	To find fault with and remove from public view	censure	Condemning as wrong; strong disapproval
cloths	Pieces of fabric	clothes	Wearing apparel
desert	A dry region; to leave or to abandon	dessert	The final course of a meal
elicit	To draw forth	illicit	Not allowed by law or custom
emigrate	To move away from; to leave a country	immigrate	To move toward; to enter a country
example	Something selected to show the nature or character of the rest	sample	A part or piece taken or shown as representative of the whole thing
human	Viewed as distinctive of people	humane	Having the best qualities of human beings
later	After some time	latter	The second of two
loose	Free; not close together; not fastened	lose	To mislay, become unable to find
moral	Good, virtuous	morale	Spirit, mental condition
persecute	To attack or to annoy someone constantly	prosecute	To bring legal action against someone for unlawful behavior
personal	Individual, private	personnel	A group of people employed in the same work or service
quiet	Still; silent	quite	Completely, rather, very
than	Conjunction used for comparisons	then	At that time; next

Table 5-2 Homonyms

aisle	Passageway between sections of seats in rows	isle	Island
all ready	All prepared	already	Previously
all together	Everyone in the same place	altogether	Entirely
altar	A table or stand at which religious rites are performed	alter	To change
boar	A mature, uncastrated male pig	bore	A tiresome, dull person or thing; to make a hole in or through with a drill
born	Given birth	borne	Carried; endured
brake	To slow down or stop; a device for slowing down or stopping	break	To cause to come apart; to shatter; a fracture
capital	City; wealth; punishable by death	capitol	A building in which a legislature meets
coarse	Rough, crude	course	Path of action; part of a meal; series of studies
complement	Something that makes whole or complete; to make whole or complete	compliment	Praise; a courteous act or expression; to express praise or respect
consul	A person appointed by a government to serve its citizens in a foreign country	council	A group called together to accomplish a purpose
		counsel	Advice; to advise
councilor	A member of a council	counselor	One who gives advice
fair	Just and honest; unblemished; clean	fare	To happen, result; money paid for transportation in a train, taxi, etc.
hole	An opening in or through anything	whole	Containing all the parts or elements

its	Possessive form of "it"	it's	Contraction of "it is" or "it has"
lead	A heavy metal; graphite in a pencil	led	Past tense of "to lead"
loan	Given for temporary use or service	lone	To be by oneself; solitary
mail	Letters, packages, papers to be handled, transported, or delivered	male	Consisting of men or boys
miner	A worker in a mine	minor	A person under legal age; less important
pain	A sensation of hurting or strong discomfort	pane	A sheet of glass in a frame
passed	Went beyond	past	Time gone by; of a former time; beyond
peace	Calmness	piece	A part of something
plain	Not fancy; clear; an area of flat land	plane	A flat surface; a tool; an airplane
principal	The head of a school; main or most	principle	A rule of conduct; a fact or a general truth
sail	A shaped sheet of canvas used to deflect wind on a land vehicle or sea vessel	sale	The act of offering goods or services for a set amount of money
sight	A view, look, or glimpse; to take aim	site	The place where something is or was
stationary	In a fixed position	stationery	Writing paper
their	Possessive form of "they"	there	At that place
		they're	Contraction of "they are"
to	Preposition; part of the infinitive form of a verb	too	Also; more than enough
		two	Totaling one plus one
waist	The midsection of the body	waste	Unused material; to squander
who's	Contraction of "who is" or "who has"	whose	Possessive form of "who"
wring	To squeeze, press, or twist so as to force out water by this means	ring	The sound of a bell; a small, circular band; to surround or encircle
your	Possessive form of "you"	you're	Contraction of "you are"

Homonyms Checkup Quiz

Underline the correct word in each sentence below *without* consulting the words in Table 5-2. Answers appear at the end of this chapter.

1. The newest addition to our exercise room is a (stationary, stationery) bicycle that is easily adjusted to different levels of muscle resistance.
2. Those who profess that "flattery will get you nowhere" also have difficulty accepting sincere (complements, compliments) from true admirers.
3. Should you run into difficulty when visiting a foreign nation, contact the office of the United States (council, counsel) before you panic.
4. The (principal, principle) issue under consideration is how to provide health care for everyone in the nation.
5. A new business requires substantial startup (capital, capitol) to survive in the first critical months.

Look-Alike Words—Homographs

Words that are spelled alike and often sound alike but have different meanings are even more confusing. Such words do not follow a specific pattern, for homograph pairs may be of the same part of speech, such as "pump" ("a type of shoe" *or* "a machine used to compress or raise liquids and gases"), or of different parts of speech, such as "bow" ("to incline the body" *or* "a ribbon with two or more loops"). Those homographs such as "bow" and "bow" that are not pronounced the same are sometimes called "heteronyms." Table 5-3 lists a number of sometimes-confused homographs.

Table 5-3 **Homographs**

Homograph	Use as a Noun or Adjective	Use as a Verb
bow	A ribbon with two or more loops	To incline the body
	A device for shooting arrows, made out of a flexible, curved piece of wood	
	A device for playing on a musical instrument of the violin or viol family, made out of a flexible curved piece of wood	

coast	Land bordering the sea	To ride down hill
lead	A heavy metal	To conduct or guide
	An act of directing or guiding	
maroon	Dark red color	To leave in a helpless position
organ	Part of a living thing	
	A musical instrument	
pen	A small enclosure	To enclose in a limited space
	A writing instrument	To write
pole	A long, slender object	
	Either end of the earth's axis	
pump	A type of shoe	To raise or lower levels of water or other liquids by using a pump
	A machine used to compress or raise liquids or gases	
roll	A type of bread	To turn over and over
slough	A swamp	To shed or to cast off
steer	Type of cattle	To turn or to direct
stern	Severe, harsh	
	The rear end of a ship or boat	
tears	Water shed from the eyes	Rips apart
	The gaps resulting when cloth is pulled apart violently	
wind	Movement of air	To turn or crank, as to wind a clock's mechanism
		To coil or curve

Homographs Checkup Quiz

Underline the phrase following each sentence below that best matches the meaning of the word that appears in italics in the sentence. Do *not* consult the words in Table 5-3. Answers appear at the end of the chapter.

1. The high winds and heavy flooding motivated many residents of Bound Brook to buy *pumps* in record numbers.

(A) a type of shoe
   (B) a machine used to compress or raise liquids or gases
2. The donation of the *organ* helped to breathe new life into the ailing congregation.
   (A) part of a living thing
   (B) a musical instrument
3. Early hunters depended on the *bow* as an instrument for gathering food and as a weapon.
   (A) a ribbon with two or more loops
   (B) a device for shooting arrows that is made out of a flexible, curved piece of wood
4. Even after we restored the ball gown to its former glory, we believed that we could still see the *tears* that had once stained the lovely satin bodice and marred the full skirt.
   (A) water shed from the eyes
   (B) the gaps resulting when cloth is pulled apart violently
5. Politicians often complain about "the tyranny of the *pen*" when they find their secrets exposed and their hidden lives revealed.
   (A) a small enclosure
   (B) a writing instrument

ANSWERS TO THE CHECKUP QUIZZES

Imposter Words

   1. morale   2. than   3. quite   4. affect   5. censure

Homonyms

   1. stationary   2. compliments   3. counsel   4. principal   5. capital

Homographs

   1B. a machine used to compress or raise liquids or gases. 2B. a musical instrument. 3B. a device for shooting arrows that is made out of a flexible, curved piece of wood. 4A. water shed from the eyes. 5B. a writing instrument.

Now that you have developed a range of ways to identify word meanings and to decide what the context calls for, let's move to the type of SAT item that students dread most—the analogy. Take a deep breath and get ready to face your analogy phobia!

Chapter 6

Analogies

Avoiding Analogy Phobia

Are you afraid of analogies? Do you avoid the analogy items on the SAT verbal section, saving them until you have completed the other items? If so, you are not alone. Many students dread analogies—and far too many students either skip those sections altogether or simply make no effort because they believe that their answers will be incorrect, no matter what they do.

How important are the analogies to your SAT verbal score? Very. The verbal section contains from 78 to 80 items. Most of the items (from 40 to 42) are questions on the critical reading sections, 19 to 20 items are sentence completions, and the remaining items (18 to 19) are analogies. One-fourth of your SAT verbal section score depends upon your ability to respond to the analogy items. You can achieve a *passable* score without doing well on the analogies section—as long as you excel in sentence completions and reading comprehension. But if you are reading this book, you don't want only a merely passable score. You are aiming for a high score, so let's begin.

What Do Analogy Items Require?

Success in correctly completing analogies depends on two skills: word knowledge and relationship recognition. You have already begun to build a large and varied vocabulary by learning many of the prefixes, roots, and suffixes that create a large number of words. Knowing how homographs and homonyms can confuse context clues will also provide the needed word knowledge skills.

Analogies ask you to find the relationship between two words, which we will call the *main word pair* throughout this book, and then to use that relationship to choose a pair of words that have the same relationship. At its simplest, the analogy relationship may be between either words that are similar (*synonyms*) or words and their opposites (*antonyms*), but many more specific relationships exist. Learning to identify those relationships will banish your analogy phobia forever.

The examples in this and the chapters that follow will focus on strengthening your ability to identify the relationships between words and to understand the many different relationships that exist. Because this is the goal, most of the examples will use everyday words—not so-called "SAT words"—to keep the emphasis on the word relationships and not send you to look up the vocabulary.

Stop being an analogy-phobe. Learn to master analogies, instead, by learning the secrets of their relationships.

Approaching Analogy Questions

Although you will face many different analogy relationships, you should approach all of them in the same way until you have identified a relationship that requires special treatment. In general, several rules can be applied:

1. The parts of speech of the words in the main word pair will be the same as the parts of speech in each of the answer-choice word pairs. For example, if the main word pair contains a noun and a verb, then all the answer choices will consist of a noun and a verb.

2. The correct answer in an analogy item must express the same relationship as that in the main word pair in the item. Further, the relationship must be expressed with words that are in the same word order as the capitalized words. If the answer choices contain a word pair that is in *reverse* word order, then you can immediately eliminate that answer as a possibility.

   Example
   NIGHT : DARK ::
   (A) music : discordant
   (B) light : morning
   (C) summer : cold
   (D) water : frozen
   (E) winter : dreary

   In the example above, a noun is paired with an adjective in the main word pair and in all the answer choices, and the noun appears first in the main word pair. When you review the choices carefully, you see that in answer choice (B) the adjective appears first in the pair, while the noun is the first word in all the other answer pairs. Not so coincidentally, the answer choice that contains the words reversed seems to be a very good match to the relationship in the main word pair: "night" and "dark" are significantly related as are "light" and "morning." Despite their matching concepts, however, choice (B) is incorrect because the words are in reverse order; thus, they express a different relationship from that expressed in the main word pair. [The correct answer, in case you are wondering, is choice (E).]

3. Before attempting to find the correct answer choice, you should first create a sentence that expresses a clear relationship between the two words in the main word pair. The more specific and necessary the relationship, the more likely will be your chance of selecting the correct answer choice. Consider this analogy:

Example

HORN : AUTOMOBILE ::

(A) propeller : helicopter

(B) whistle : train

(C) engine : bus

(D) wing : airplane

(E) wheel : wagon

If we create a sentence that expresses the relationship between the words in the main word pair, we might say that "A HORN is a component part of an AUTOMOBILE." The relationship appears to have been stated in a sufficiently specific manner, until we then try the words in each of the other pairs and find that *all* the answer choices seem to complete the relationship sentence accurately.

(A) A *propeller* is a component part of a *helicopter*.

(B) A *whistle* is a component part of a *train*.

(C) An *engine* is a component part of a *bus*.

(D) A *wing* is a component part of an *airplane*.

(E) A *wheel* is a component part of a *wagon*.

What you must do in this case is to make the relationship between the main words even more specific.

Consider what function a horn has on an automobile. Not only is the horn a piece of the equipment of an automobile, but it is the piece of equipment that is used to alert other drivers to the oncoming automobile. Create a new, more specific relationship sentence:

A HORN is a component part of an AUTOMOBILE used to warn others of its approach.

Now, insert the word pairs of each of the answer choices into the new, more specific relationship sentence.

(A) A *propeller* is a component part of a *helicopter* used to warn others of its approach.

(B) A *whistle* is a component part of a *train* used to warn others of its approach.

(C) An *engine* is a component part of a *bus* used to warn others of its approach.

(D) A *wing* is a component part of an *airplane* used to warn others of its approach.

(E) A *wheel* is a component part of a *wagon* used to warn others of its approach.

The sentences that result show that choices (A), (C), (D), and (E) fail to result in true statements. Only choice (B) exhibits the same true relationship as that of the main word pair, because the function of a whistle on a train is to warn others of the approach of the train.

4. Use the process of elimination to narrow your choices to two of the answer pairs. First, eliminate any answer pairs that contain the parts of speech in reverse order, as well as those in which the words in the pair have no connection to each other. Next, test the remaining pairs to remove those having only a weak connection. If you are fortunate, this process will leave only one choice—the correct answer. If not, then rewrite the sentence containing the main word pair to make the relationship more specific and necessary.

5. If the steps do not produce a clear choice, then circle the item in the booklet and the two choices you are debating and move on to the remaining items. If you do not feel confident enough to make an educated guess, then do not risk an incorrect answer at that time. You can always return to the item after completing the remaining items in the section.

6. After recording all the answers in which you have confidence, return to those that you circled. You may find that contemplating the connections between word pairs in other items has given you a different perspective that makes one of the debated choices clearly the correct choice.

General Analogies Quiz

Each of the following questions consists of a related pair of words followed by five pairs of words labeled A through E. Select the pair of words whose relationship is the same as the relationship of the pair in capital letters.

1. BLOWTORCH : WELD ::
   (A)   paper : tape
   (B)   define : dictionary
   (C)   frog : hop
   (D)   needle : cloth
   (E)   stapler : attach

2. DEDICATION : DEVOTION ::
   (A)   flavor : smell
   (B)   end : means
   (C)   intention : purpose
   (D)   hate : love
   (E)   dilatory : punctual

3. ORIGINAL : REPRODUCTION ::
   (A)   interested : intrigued
   (B)   perfect : defective
   (C)   pure : clean
   (D)   old : elderly
   (E)   cracked : molded

4. BOAT : CANOE ::
   (A)   car : truck
   (B)   wheel : wagon
   (C)   mast : boat
   (D)   transportation : train
   (E)   rose : flower

5. NECK : BODY ::
   (A)   sail : anchor
   (B)   mane : horse
   (C)   steam : engine
   (D)   mast : boat
   (E)   wasp : stinger

6. SALUTATION : FAREWELL ::
   (A)   plane : bus
   (B)   friendship : anger
   (C)   noon : midnight
   (D)   birth : death
   (E)   army : navy

7. CONCEAL : REVEAL ::
   (A)   mount : ascend
   (B)   sail : navigate
   (C)   sink : swim
   (D)   emerge : withdraw
   (E)   submerge : surface

8. BABY : INFANT ::
   (A)   boy : girl
   (B)   judge : jury
   (C)   cow : calf
   (D)   teenager : youth
   (E)   kitten : cat

9. UNDERSTANDING : COMPREHENSION ::
   (A) hate : love
   (B) tranquility : serenity
   (C) dignity : ridicule
   (D) contempt : scorn
   (E) morning : evening

10. SHORT : TALL ::
    (A) ridiculous : laughable
    (B) blunt : sharp
    (C) bizarre : outrageous
    (D) question : query
    (E) novelty : innovation

ANSWERS TO THE GENERAL ANALOGIES QUIZ

To determine the correct relationship, place the capitalized words into the form of a sentence that expresses a clear and necessary relationship. Then test the answer choices by inserting the words in each pair in that sentence.

1. BLOWTORCH : WELD
   (A) paper : tape
   (B) define : dictionary
   (C) frog : hop
   (D) needle : cloth
   (E) stapler : attach

   Explanation: If you place the capitalized words into a sentence that expresses a clear relationship between them, the following statement results:

   A BLOWTORCH is used to WELD items together.

   Thus,
   (A) A *paper* is used to *tape* items together.
   (B) A *define* is used to *dictionary* items together.
   (C) A *frog* is used to *hop* items together.
   (D) A *needle* is used to *cloth* items together.
   (E) A *stapler* is used to *attach* items together.

   Among the above sentences, choices (A), (B), (C), and (D) offer no meaningful relationships. Only choice (E) provides an answer that correctly relates the word pair, because a stapler really does attach items.

2. DEDICATION : DEVOTION
   (A) flavor : smell
   (B) end : means
   (C) intention : purpose

(D) hate : love
(E) dilatory : punctual

Explanation: If you place the capitalized words into a sentence that expresses a clear relationship between them, the following statement results:

To have DEDICATION is also to have DEVOTION to someone or something.

Thus,

- (A) To have *flavor* is also to have *smell*.
- (B) To have an *end* is also to have *means*.
- (C) To have an *intention* is also to have a *purpose*.
- (D) To show *hate* is also to show *love*.
- (E) To be *dilatory* is also to be *punctual*.

Among the above sentences, choice (A) offers no meaningful relationship, and choices (B), (D), and (E) present opposite relationships. Only choice (C) provides an answer that correctly relates the word pair, because to have an intention is the same as having a purpose.

3. ORIGINAL : REPRODUCTION
   - (A) interested : intrigued
   - (B) perfect : defective
   - (C) pure : clean
   - (D) old : elderly
   - (E) cracked : molded

Explanation: If you place the capitalized words into a sentence that expresses a clear relationship between them, the following statement results:

An ORIGINAL is the opposite of a REPRODUCTION.

Thus,

- (A) To be *interested* is the opposite of being *intrigued*.
- (B) To be *perfect* is the opposite of being *defective*.
- (C) To be *pure* is the opposite of being *clean*.
- (D) To be *old* is the opposite of being *elderly*.
- (E) To be *cracked* is the opposite of being *molded*.

Among the above sentences, choice (E) offers no meaningful relationship, and choices (A), (C), and (D) present words that mean the same. Only choice (B) provides an answer that correctly relates the word pair, because to be perfect is the opposite of being defective.

4. BOAT : CANOE
    (A) car : truck
    (B) wheel : wagon
    (C) mast : boat
    (D) transportation : train
    (E) rose : flower

   Explanation: If you place the capitalized words into a sentence that expresses a clear relationship between them, the following statement results:

   A CANOE is a type of BOAT.
   Thus,
   (A) A *truck* is a type of *car*.
   (B) A *wagon* is a type of *wheel*.
   (C) A *boat* is a type of *mast*.
   (D) A *train* is a type of *transportation*.
   (E) A *flower* is a type of *rose*.

   Among the above sentences, choices (A), (B), and (C) offer no meaningful relationships. Choice (E) provides two words that might relate exactly as the capitalized words, but they are in reverse order. Only choice (D) provides an answer that correctly relates the word pair, because a train is a type of transportation.

5. NECK : BODY
    (A) sail : anchor
    (B) mane : horse
    (C) steam : engine
    (D) mast : boat
    (E) wasp : stinger

   Explanation: If you place the capitalized words into a sentence that expresses a clear relationship between them, the following statement results:

A NECK extends upward from the BODY.

Thus,

- (A) A *sail* extends upward from the *anchor*.
- (B) A *mane* extends upward from the *horse*.
- (C) A *steam* extends upward from the *engine*.
- (D) A *mast* extends upward from the *boat*.
- (E) A *wasp* extends upward from the *stinger*.

Among the above sentences, choices (A), (B), (C), and (E) offer no meaningful relationships. Only choice (D) provides an answer that correctly relates the word pair, because a mast extends upward from a boat.

6. SALUTATION : FAREWELL
   - (A) plane : bus
   - (B) friendship : anger
   - (C) noon : midnight
   - (D) birth : death
   - (E) army : navy

Explanation: If you place the capitalized words into a sentence that expresses a clear relationship between them, the following statement results:

A SALUTATION (welcome) is the opposite of a FAREWELL.

Thus,

- (A) A *plane* is the opposite of a *bus*.
- (B) A *friendship* is the opposite of *anger*.
- (C) A *noon* is the opposite of *midnight*.
- (D) A *birth* is the opposite of *death*.
- (E) An *army* is the opposite of a *navy*.

Among the above sentences, choices (A), (B), and (E) offer no meaningful relationships. Choice (C) offers a possibility, but "noon" and "midnight" are not really opposites. Only choice (D) provides an answer that correctly relates the word pair, because a birth is a beginning and it is the opposite of a death, which is an ending.

7. CONCEAL : REVEAL
   - (A) mount : ascend
   - (B) sail : navigate
   - (C) sink : swim
   - (D) emerge : withdraw
   - (E) submerge : surface

   Explanation: If you place the capitalized words into a sentence that expresses a clear relationship between them, the following statement results:

   To CONCEAL is the opposite action of trying to REVEAL.

   Thus,
   - (A) To *mount* is the opposite action of trying to *ascend*.
   - (B) To *sail* is the opposite action of trying to *navigate*.
   - (C) To *sink* is the opposite action of trying to *swim*.
   - (D) To *emerge* is the opposite action of trying to *withdraw*.
   - (E) To *submerge* is the opposite action of trying to *surface*.

   Among the above sentences, choices (A) and (B) offer no meaningful relationships. Choice (C) offers a possibility, but "sink" and "swim" are not really opposites. Choice (D) offers an opposite relationship, but the words are reversed. Only choice (E) offers a correctly ordered opposite relationship, because to submerge is similar to conceal as surface is similar to reveal.

8. BABY : INFANT
   - (A) boy : girl
   - (B) judge : jury
   - (C) cow : calf
   - (D) teenager : youth
   - (E) kitten : cat

   Explanation: If you place the capitalized words into a sentence that expresses a clear relationship between them, the following statement results:

A BABY is the same as an INFANT.

Thus,

    (A)   A *boy* is the same as a *girl*.
    (B)   A *judge* is the same as a *jury*.
    (C)   A *cow* is the same as a *calf*.
    (D)   A *teenager* is the same as a *youth*.
    (E)   A *kitten* is the same as a *cat*.

Among the above sentences, choices (A), (B), (C), and (E) offer untrue relationships. Only choice (D) offers a correctly ordered similar relationship, because a teenager is the same as a youth.

9. UNDERSTANDING : COMPREHENSION
   (A) hate : love
   (B) tranquillity : serenity
   (C) dignity : ridicule
   (D) contempt : scorn
   (E) morning : evening

Explanation: If you place the capitalized words into a sentence that expresses a clear relationship between them, the following statement results:

To have UNDERSTANDING is the same as to have COMPREHENSION.

Thus,

    (A)   To have *hate* is the same as to have *love*.
    (B)   To have *tranquillity* is the same as to have *serenity*.
    (C)   To have *dignity* is the same as to have *ridicule*.
    (D)   To have *contempt* is the same as to have *scorn*.
    (E)   To have *morning* is the same as to have *evening*.

Among the above sentences, choices (A), (C), and (E) offer untrue relationships. Choice (B) expressed a true (similar) relationship. Only choice (D) offers a correctly ordered similar relationship, because to have contempt is the same as to have scorn.

10. SHORT : TALL
    (A) ridiculous : laughable
    (B) blunt : sharp
    (C) bizarre : outrageous
    (D) question : query
    (E) novelty : innovation

Explanation: If you place the capitalized words into a sentence that expresses a clear relationship between them, the following statement results:

To be SHORT is the opposite of being TALL.

Thus,
    (A) To be *ridiculous* is the opposite of being *laughable*.
    (B) To be *blunt* is the opposite of being *sharp*.
    (C) To be *bizarre* is the opposite of being *outrageous*.
    (D) To be a *question* is the opposite of being a *query*.
    (E) To be a *novelty* is the opposite of being an *innovation*.

Among the above sentences, choices (A), (C), (D), and (E) offer similar relationships, so they do not match the opposite relationship expressed by the main word pair. Only choice (B) offers a correctly ordered opposite relationship, because to be blunt is the opposite of being sharp.

Now that you have examined the most general of analogy relationships, learn to identify the specific relationships that lead to a greater understanding of analogies—and higher SAT verbal scores.

Chapter 7

Analogies

Troubleshooting

Let's get down to business and turn our attention to the problems that arise in responding to analogy items. We will first review (with some additions) the steps to successfully dealing with all analogies that you practiced in Chapter 6:

1. *Identify the parts of speech in the main word pair.* Review the answer-choice word pairs to verify the parts of speech, because the main word pair and all answer pairs should contain the same parts of speech. You will probably have to draw upon your knowledge of *homographs* and *homonyms* to determine the correct part of speech when such dual-purpose words as "pump" (noun and verb), "bow" (noun and verb), or "plain" (noun and adjective) are used.
2. *Review the answer choices to make certain that all word pairs contain the parts of speech in the same order as those in the main word pair.* Immediately eliminate any items that are in reverse word order.
3. *Before selecting an answer, create a sentence that expresses a clear relationship between the two words in the main word pair.* Make the relationship as clear and necessary as possible, so that you can identify the specific analogy relationship and apply specific skills.
4. *Narrow your choices to two of the answer pairs by using the process of elimination.* Ignore as answers any choices that place the parts of speech in reverse word order as well as those word pairs that have no connection with each other.
5. *Do not waste too much time on any one analogy item.* If you find yourself spending a minute pondering, yet not making a clear answer choice, stop and return later to the item. Circle the item in your SAT booklet, circle the two or three possible answers, and then move on.

6. *After recording all the answers in which you have confidence, return to those that you circled.* Make an educated guess if you have narrowed your choices to only two. You will only lose 1/4 point if your answer is incorrect, but you will gain 1 point if it is correct.

When You Don't Know the Parts of Speech

To determine more specific analogy relationships, which makes your task of choosing the correct answer easier, add to the general approach to analogies. What can you do if the relationship of the words in the main word pair is not immediately evident?

Work backward!

You already know that all the answer choices in an analogy item *must* contain the same parts of speech as the main word pair, so examine the answer choices to help you to decide how the words in the main word pair are used. If you can determine definitely the parts of speech and their order in two of the five answer choices, then you can confidently name the parts of speech and their order in the main word pair.

Example

FLY : INSECT ::

(A) frog : toad

(B) horse : race

(C) swallow : bird

(D) dog : cat

(E) lion : tiger

The main word pair in the example presents a difficulty, because "fly" might be either an action or a type of insect. Before you can form a sentence that states a clear and necessary relationship, you will have to decide how the word "fly" is used—as a noun or as a verb. Because all the answer choices in the analogies that appear in the SAT verbal section must contain the same parts of speech, reviewing the choices should reveal the parts of speech of the specific analogy item. Choice (A) contains a clear pairing of two nouns, "frog" and "toad," as does choice (E), "lion" and "tiger." Choice (B) contains the definite noun "horse," but "race" can be either a noun or a verb. Choice (C) contains the definite noun "bird," but "swallow" can be either a noun or a verb.

Choice (D) contains two words that are usually used as nouns, but they are also used as verbs, i.e., to "dog" (to hunt or to track down) and to "cat" (to raise anchor to the cathead, the projecting beam of wood near the bow on a ship). Because two of the choices consist indisputably of noun pairs, however, we can confidently decide that all the answer choices *and* the main word pair are noun pairs.

Armed with that knowledge, after working backward, you can now create a sentence that identifies a clear and meaningful relationship using the main word pair:

A FLY is a specific type of INSECT.

(A) A *frog* is a specific type of *toad.*

(B) A *horse* is a specific type of *race.*

(C) A *swallow* is a specific type of *bird.*

(D) A *dog* is a specific type of *cat.*

(E) A *lion* is a specific type of *tiger.*

You can eliminate choices (A), (B), (D), and (E) as being untrue, leaving choice (C) as your answer.

When You Don't Know the Main Word Pair Meanings

The above procedure solves one of your problems, but what can you do if you do not know the meaning of one or both of the main-pair words? How can you determine the relationships between the words if you do not know what the words mean?

Work backward!

When stumped by the meaning of one or both words in the main word pair, use the answer choices to help you determine what they mean or what the answer might be. Doing so will aid you in making an educated guess that will probably be correct. Even if you do not know the meanings of all the answer-choice words, you do know that only one of the answers is correct. In some cases, one of the answer word pairs will stand apart from the remaining four by being either related when the others are opposites or opposite when the other are related, specific when the others are general or general when the others are specific, and so on. The correct choice is easily made in this situation. Of course, you cannot count on the solution being so easy in most instances. Instead, you will have to examine each of the answer choices to determine which contain meaningful relationships between the paired words.

Example

SAD : LUGUBRIOUS ::

(A)   mandatory : voluntary

(B)   malicious : beneficial

(C)   talkative : profitable

(D)   eager : zealous

(E)   colorful : colorless

Do you know the meaning of the word "lugubrious" in the main word pair of the example? Most people do not. Even if you do, let's pretend that you don't as we use the above example to guide you through working backward to answer an analogy question. Begin by identifying what you do know about the main word pair and the answer choices. We can go about this in several ways.

You know that one word in the main word pair is an adjective—"sad" works as no other part of speech—so you can be confident in believing that at least one word in each of the answer choices is also an adjective. Now turn to the answer choices. If at least one word in each pair must be an adjective, identify that one word first before examining the second word for its part of speech. Look for an answer choice that contains words you know. The easiest in this example is choice (E). Both "colorful" and "colorless" are adjectives—and both function *only* as adjectives, and so we can expect that all the answer choices *and* the main word pair contain two adjectives.

The next step is to determine if a strong specific relationship exists between word pairs in the answer choices. Because you do not know the meanings of both main-pair words, you cannot create a sentence that exhibits a clear and meaningful relationship between them and then test the answer choices by inserting words into the sentence. Instead, you must determine the relationship that exists within each pair of words, possibly with a different sentence for each.

Choice (A)   Something that is *mandatory* is not *voluntary*.

Choice (B)   Something that is *malicious* is not *beneficial*.

Choice (C)   Something that is *talkative* has no relationship to being *profitable*.

Choice (D)   Something that is *eager* is also *zealous*.

Choice (E)   Something that is *colorful* is not *colorless*.

In the example, choice (C) exhibits no relationship between the two words, and so we can easily eliminate this choice from consideration.

Even so, we are faced with a problem, because choices (A), (B), and (E) contain equally clear and strong *opposite* relationships. This very fact, however, makes the choice of any one of the three unlikely because they are too similar in strength and, thus, pose no means of differentiating among them. By the process of elimination—and without even considering meaning—we are left with choice (D), eager : zealous. The word pair contains two words that differ only in intensity. "Eager" means to "feel or to show desire," while "zealous" means to "show ardent devotion." When we consult a dictionary for the meaning of "lugubrious," we learn that its meaning is "very sad or mournful." Thus, choice (D) correctly reflects the relationship of the main word pair.

Will the above approaches work in responding to all difficult analogy items? Probably not. Do not look at them as a substitute for increasing your word knowledge and building vocabulary. Instead, consider them to be emergency measures that you will apply when all else fails.

Chapter 8

Analogy Types

Size and Degree

Let's get down to business and turn our attention to conquering specific types of analogies. The SAT verbal section does not categorize analogies by type, but you should. Knowing the specific relationship between the words in the main word pair allows you to apply specific skills—skills that you will learn in this chapter and in the three chapters that follow.

The most easily visualized types of analogies are those in which size is compared, units are measured, and degrees of intensity are determined—after we recognize that such comparisons are being sought. Although they are no more difficult than other analogy types, we tend to overlook the relationships that they represent or to see them in less specific terms. In this chapter, you will sharpen your observation skills to help you in identifying these specific relationships in analogy items.

Relating Size

You must be careful in identifying size relationships that you do not confuse them with measurement or degree-of-intensity relationships. In general, this type of analogy relates either something smaller in size to something larger in size or something larger in size to something smaller in size. Either way, the issue of measurement is not a concern in this specific relationship. The items being compared are related according to the percentage or ratio that one is of the other. In essence, the comparison is relative rather than exact.

Example

COTTAGE : MANSION ::

(A)   giant : dwarf

(B)   man : woman

(C)   desk : chair

(D)   bed : couch

(E)   mouse : elephant

Approach: Both words in the main word pair name buildings. A cottage is a small structure, no more than two stories in height, built to serve as a personal home. In contrast, a mansion is a very large structure with many more rooms than a cottage, although it is also built to serve as someone's home. The difference here, however, is in the size, and so we should use size as the basis for comparison in evaluating the answer choices. Begin by constructing a sentence that expresses a meaningful relationship between the two structures. "A COTTAGE is a smaller home than a MANSION." Now test the answer choices to see which contain a similar relationship.

A COTTAGE is a smaller home than a MANSION.

(A)   A *giant* is a smaller person than a *dwarf.*

(B)   A *man* is a smaller person than a *woman.*

(C)   A *desk* is a smaller piece of furniture than a *chair.*

(D)   A *bed* is a smaller piece of furniture than a *couch.*

(E)   A *mouse* is a smaller animal than an *elephant.*

You can immediately eliminate choice (A), because the terms are reversed and a giant is actually *larger* than a dwarf. Choice (B) provides no relationship because men and women are different sizes and some women are larger than some men. Choice (C) is more likely reversed, because a desk is usually larger than a chair, but it does not have to be, and so no relationship exists. Choice (D) provides no relationship, because of the vast differences in sizes of both objects. Only choice (E) clearly and accurately compares the mouse to the elephant, because a mouse *is* a smaller animal than an elephant.

Relating Units of Measurement

Analogies that deal with size relate their main word pairs according to proportion or ratio, while analogies reviewed in this section relate units of measurement to the main word pairs. [And as you review the basic equivalencies for the SAT math section, pay particular attention to the distance and weight conversions, such as the number of inches in a foot (12), the number of feet in a yard (3), and the number of feet in a mile (5,280)]. To be fully prepared for analogies that focus on units of measurement, you should also know the number of ounces in a cup (8), cups in a quart (4), and quarts in a gallon (4).

Example

LIQUID : LITERS ::

- (A) length : grams
- (B) happiness : tears
- (C) achievement : dollars
- (D) distance : miles
- (E) kilograms : weight

Approach: The main-pair words are related, because one represents the manner of measuring the other in a quantifiable manner. In other words, the relationship between "liquid" and "liters" is one that can be verified as fact, and it does not allow for the indefinite nature that opinion often interjects into analogy solutions. Thus, we can state the clear and meaningful relationship between the two main-pair words in a very simple manner by noting the following: "LIQUID is measured in units called LITERS." We must now apply this statement to the five answer choices to test the strength of their associations.

LIQUID is measured in units called LITERS.

- (A) *Length* is measured in units called *grams.*
- (B) *Happiness* is measured in units called *tears.*
- (C) *Achievement* is measured in units called *dollars.*
- (D) *Distance* is measured in units called *miles.*
- (E) *Kilograms* are measured in units called *weight.*

You can immediately eliminate choice (B), because of several reasons. Tears may be shed when people are happy, but they are more likely associated with sadness and loss. Further, tears are not a "unit of measure." Choice (C) is also eliminated because some people may measure achievement in terms of the number of dollars someone acquires, but this approach is not universally agreed upon. Choice (A) is clearly incorrect, because weight, *not* length, is measured in grams;

and choice (E) is also incorrect, because the terms are reversed and it is weight that is measured in kilograms, not the other way around. This leaves choice (D), which accurately relates the measurement of distance to miles.

Relating Degrees of Intensity

Analogies that ask you to compare items or actions according to degrees of intensity may often require a firm understanding of the sometimes fine differences between words that we carelessly use as synonyms when we speak and write. Consider when you and someone do not think the same way about an issue and the result is that both of you express differing opinions with passion. Are you likely to say that you "disagreed," "argued," "clashed"? If you feel that the two of you *argued* but your friend feels that the two of you *disagreed*, might you not have unfinished business with which to deal? The distance in emotional response that exists between disagreeing and arguing is great. Not only do such differences of perspective make personal relationships tense, but they also make for some tense times when facing the analogies section of the SAT verbal section.

How can you sharpen your understanding of the shades of meaning that often arise among words? Begin now to speak and to write as specifically as possible, using the *exact* term rather than just a *good-enough* term. The student who races to class rather than runs to class shows a greater intensity of movement, so select your words carefully to convey the exact thought with the most specific description. Such everyday attention to being specific will pay off when you face analogy items that relate to degrees of intensity.

Example
DRIZZLE : DOWNPOUR ::

(A) mountain : earthquake

(B) lake : puddle

(C) river : stream

(D) breeze : hurricane

(E) flurry : avalanche

Approach: Both items in the main word pair relate to rainfall in varying degrees. A "drizzle" is light rainfall that may be barely felt, while a "downpour" is a heavy rainfall that may have significant effects. Thus, the relationship between the words in the main pair is one of intensity, in which the first word in the pair is of lesser intensity than the second word in the pair: "A DRIZZLE is a lesser form of rainfall than a DOWNPOUR." We must now apply this relationship to the five answer choices to identify the one choice that best matches the relationship in the main word pair.

A DRIZZLE is a lesser form of rainfall than a DOWNPOUR.

(A) A *mountain* is a lesser form of land mass than an *earthquake*.
(B) A *lake* is a lesser body of water than a *puddle*.
(C) A *river* is a lesser body of water than a *stream*.
(D) A *breeze* is a lesser form of air than a *hurricane*.
(E) A *flurry* is a lesser form of snowfall than an *avalanche*.

After reviewing the relationship sentences, you can immediately eliminate choices (A) and (E). In choice (A), a mountain is a land form but an earthquake is not, and so comparison between the two in regard to intensity or degree of difference is irrelevant. In choice (E), a flurry is a form of snowfall, a very light snowfall, but an avalanche is the *result* of snowfall and not a form of snowfall. Choices (B) and (C) offer the relationship between two types of body of water that differ in degree. The difference is that a puddle is a lesser form of a body of water than a lake, and a stream is a lesser form of a body of water than a river—not the other way around as the relationship stated in the main word pair requires. Choice (D) offers the only relationship that correctly matches the relationship of degree of intensity that is expressed in the main word pair.

Knowing the specific analogy relationships will give you an edge in approaching the analogy items on the SAT, and so continue to the next chapter where you will examine how to classify and identify characteristics of people, objects, or places.

Chapter 9

Analogy Types

Classifications and Characteristics

The analogy relationships that depend upon classifications and identifying characteristics are not as straightforward as these two categories seem to suggest. Instead, they are rather broad, because their range is so diverse. You classify objects and ideas when you associate specific qualities or conditions with them and when you show how some objects and ideas affect other objects and ideas. You are also dealing with relationships of classification and identifying characteristics when you relate actions to the objects that are acted upon or are the result of that action and when you create analogous relationships between a tool and the object or the activity it is used for. Integral to this area of analogy study is also the more obvious use of classification in regard to animals, according to gender classifications, group relationships, and parent-offspring categories. Rather than a simple area of study, the examination of analogy relationships that depend upon classification and characteristics requires a good deal of your attention both to grasp the differences among categories and to add new vocabulary that will provide you with the means of expressing and understanding those categories.

Relating Objects and Ideas to Specific Qualities or Conditions

Certain qualities are often associated with specific actions or types of behavior, and the associations may be either positive or negative. In like manner, we automatically attach adjectives to nouns in ways that may reveal more about our social conditioning and cultural training than about the nouns themselves. This last action creates serious difficulty for many who respond personally to the analogy items on the SAT verbal section, because they fail to take into account that the assessment tool is used nationwide and requires a societywide, rather than a culturally narrow, point of view.

Example

MEMORY : ELUSIVE ::

(A) savory : taste
(B) melodious : hearing
(C) fame : fleeting
(D) blurred : vision
(E) touch : rough

Approach: The main word pair and the five answer choices team nouns with the qualities that *might* be associated with them. Let's begin with a sentence that expresses the meaningful relationship between the main-word-pair items. "MEMORY that fades is said to be ELUSIVE." In essence, this association reflects one of many associated qualities of memory, but it is not an essential quality. Therefore, we must assess the answer choices in the same manner.

MEMORY that fades is said to be ELUSIVE.

Savory that fades is said to *taste*.

Melodious that fades is said to be *hearing*.

Fame that fades is said to be *fleeting*.

Blurred that fades is said to be *vision*.

Touch that fades is said to be *rough*.

Even before placing all the choices into the relationship sentence, you could have eliminated choices (A), (B), and (D) from consideration. The order of the word parts in the main word pair relates the noun "memory" to the adjective "elusive," but the adjectives appear first in these three choices. Had the words been reversed in choice (D), so that the sentence might have read, "*Vision* that fades is said to be *blurred*," the result would have been a strong contender for the correct answer. As it is, only choices (C) and (E) contain word pairs ordered like the main word pair. Choice (E) is also eliminated, however, because touch that fades may be imperceptible, but it is not rough. Thus, choice (C) is the correct answer, because it provides the same relationship as the main word pair.

ANOTHER EXAMPLE—OBJECTS

Objects may also be related to an essential quality or condition in this specific analogy relationship. When relating words in this manner, we depend upon socially established values and conditions related to objects. Therefore, we expect that a church should be religious, gold is valuable, a mystery is puzzling, an arbitrator should be impartial, and a teacher should be an educator. Many other expectations exist based upon definitions that we have for ideas and objects.

Example

LOGIC : RATIONAL ::

- (A) flowers : beautiful
- (B) religious : church
- (C) impartial : arbitrator
- (D) mystery : puzzling
- (E) joke : humorous

Approach: Begin by creating a sentence that places the main word pair into a meaningful and clear relationship. Then place the words from the answer choices into the same sentence.

LOGIC must be RATIONAL.

Flowers must be *beautiful*.

A *religious* must be a *church*.

An *impartial* must be an *arbitrator*.

A *mystery* must be *puzzling*.

A *joke* must be *humorous*.

Choices (B) and (C) can immediately be eliminated, because the noun and adjective in each item are reversed, even if the relationships between the words in each pair are similar to that in the main word pair. You can also eliminate choices (A) and (E), because flowers are not always beautiful nor are jokes always humorous. Thus, choice (D) is correct, because by definition a mystery *is* puzzling.

Relating Objects or Ideas to Other Objects or Ideas

The relationships in this specific analogy category cover time relationships, goal and purpose, and that which does or does not exist but should between two ideas or objects. In some cases, your familiarity with an idea or object will make the relationship seem to be obvious, while in other instances you will search your mind long and hard to see even the hint of a relationship. If this difficulty arises, you may have to broaden your thinking to consider additional possibilities. In some cases, you will have to call upon your skills in determining the part of speech being played by a word.

Example

PRUNE : FRUIT TREES::

(A)   lawn : mow

(B)   plow : soil

(C)   wash : clothes

(D)   grow : vegetables

(E)   wheat : harvest

Approach: The time has arrived for you to save a few seconds even in practice, and so do not create and apply a word sentence to the answer choices until *after* you have eliminated all the obviously wrong answers. The main word pair relates the verb to the noun, but choices (A) and (E) reverse the word order, and so they can be eliminated immediately. The remaining choices all contain actions that one might undertake. As you might prune the fruit trees, you can also plow the soil, wash the clothes, and grow the vegetables. Because all three choices are possible actions, you must make the relationship sentence using the main word pair more specific. What does it mean to prune fruit trees? What action does it entail? The action of pruning requires cutting branches of a tree to make it more fruitful, and the action of plowing requires cutting into the soil to prepare it to become more fertile. Thus, the correct choice is (B).

ANOTHER EXAMPLE—NEGATIVE ASSOCIATION

Another type of relationship might be a negative association in which a lack of the object named is related to the result of taking away that object rather than the more positive association. Some possible negative associations include *the lack of stress that might associated with equilibrium, the lack of laughter that might be associated with somber behavior,* or *the lack of money that might be associated with poverty,* among many others.

Example

SLEEP : EXHAUSTION::

(A) boredom : challenge

(B) contentment : success

(C) poverty : money

(D) air : suffocation

(E) work : recreation

   Approach: You cannot eliminate any answer choices due to reversed order of the parts of speech, and so you must create a sentence that identifies a meaningful and clear relationship between the main word parts and then apply it to the answer choices. The relationship between sleep and exhaustion appears to be the following: "The lack of SLEEP results in EXHAUSTION."

   When you substitute the choice (A) word pair, you find that the relationship is reversed, because the lack of boredom does not result in challenge, but the lack of challenge results in boredom. Choice (C) offers a possible relationship between poverty and money, but the words are also reversed, and choices (B) and (E) offer no relationships because the lack of contentment does not necessarily result in success, nor does the lack of work necessarily result in recreation. Choice (D) is correct because a lack of air does result in suffocation.

Relating Actions and Objects

You will have to determine object-action relationships of several types in analogy items. Some will simply ask that you determine the relationship between an object and its usual use, while others may require that you identify the usual activity of the object and the result of that activity.

Example

HOOP : BASKETBALL ::

(A) base : baseball

(B) goalposts : football

(C) stove : cooking

(D) rifle : hunting

(E) tutu : ballet

Approach: Review the answer choices and you will see that all are possible correct answers if we simply state of the main word pair that: "A HOOP is used in the activity of BASKETBALL." To create a more specific relationship, the relationship of the hoop to the goal of the game of basketball must be identified. Of what importance is the hoop? How does it relate to basketball—or to *the* basketball? This is where our concern must lie. We must use the term "basketball" to mean the object, and not the game, if we are to create a more specific and meaningful statement. When we do so, the following statement results: "The BASKETBALL passes through the HOOP to score points." When we substitute the answer choices in this statement, we can immediately eliminate choices (A), (C), (D), and (E). Although all the pairs contain related words, none contain the relationship that will result in scoring points except for choice (B): "The football passes through the goalposts to score points." In the game of football, other means exist to score points, but this is one of the ways and the *best* answer among the choices.

Gender, Group, and Parent-Offspring Classification

Analogies also ask that you relate animals according to their gender ("cow-bull," "mare-stallion," "ram-ewe," "gander-goose"), group name (a "herd" of cattle, a "murder" of crows, a "flock" of sheep, a "pride" of lions, a "pack" of wolves), or their parent-offspring categories ("mare-foal," "cat-kitten," "dog-puppy," "cow-calf," "bear-cub," "goose-gosling"). For the most part, these relationships are easily identified, as long as you know the vocabulary that names the category or relationship. You must also remain aware of the homographs that are used deliberately to test your word knowledge and reasoning abilities.

Example

LIONS : PRIDE ::

(A) cattle : cow

(B) pigs : litter

(C) sheep : flock

(D) tigers : fierceness

(E) pack : wolves

Approach: The analogy includes a trick for those who are not aware that the group within which lions travel is called a "pride." Therefore, you must compose a meaningful and clear sentence that exhibits this relationship: "LIONS travel in a group called a PRIDE." When you review the answer choices, you find that all relate noun to noun, as we see in the main word group, although such words as "litter," "flock," and "pack" might also be used as verbs. When we insert the answer choices into the relationship sentence, we find that we can immediately eliminate choice (A), because "cattle" is a plural form of "cow," not the group in which cows move. Choice (B) is also eliminated, because pigs are born in a litter but they do not travel in a litter. Choice (C) is correct, because sheep do travel in a group called a "flock." And while tigers may be characterized by fierceness, a choice that might be made by someone who thought that the word "pride" in the main word group is used to mean a quality rather than a quantity, choice (D) is also incorrect. The relationship between the pack and wolves in choice (E) is correct, but the words are reversed and so the analogy is incorrect. Thus choice (C) remains the only correct choice.

The following chapter will expand your ability to respond to analogies and sharpen your ability to identify relationships that move from the general to the specific.

Chapter 10

Analogy Types

General to Specific

Many students are more comfortable when working with analogies that relate the whole to a part, a container to something contained, or a general term to a more specific term. Why? Some claim that the examples should be easier to understand, because they represent relationships between everyday actions and objects, and they expect that the analogies will contain more frequently used familiar and everyday words. For others, the possibility of concrete rather than abstract relationships—of identifying varying relationships between objects—makes this type of analogy more understandable. Easy or difficult, your mission is to master all types of analogies, and so let's begin.

Whatever your opinion, the general-to-specific analogy is an important type to master. The choices are not always obvious, and the relationships often present a considerable challenge if you choose to see only the obvious and refuse to probe beneath the surface. As with other analogy types, identifying the exact relationship between two words or concepts remains key, and the need for specificity continues to be important. You will also find that analogies of this type will force you to take a different view of what you may have once perceived to be everyday actions and objects.

Relating the Whole to the Part

Analogy items that ask you to relate the whole to the part (and the part to the whole) also draw upon your knowledge of how the components of objects relate to each other individually as well as to the greater object. What is the relationship of the diameter to a circle? Of a leaf to a tree? Of a crumb to a cookie? The relationships can be defined in regard to their usual applications, but you will probably have to modify your definitions when called upon to determine how each of these relationships relates to others in an analogy item.

Example

ROOF : HOUSE ::

(A)   desk : top
(B)   door : porch
(C)   lid : container
(D)   hair : head
(E)   apex : triangle

    Approach: Begin your analysis by creating a sentence that expresses as specifically as possible the part-to-the-whole relationship between the items in the main word pair: "The ROOF is situated at the top of a HOUSE." Simply applying this sentence to the choices, you can immediately eliminate choices (A) and (B), because the terms in the first choice are reversed and no relationship exists between the words in the second choice.

    You are now left with three choices that meet the requirements of the general relationship that you expressed. A lid is situated at the top of a container. Hair is situated at the top of a head. The apex is situated at the top of a triangle. You must now express the relationship between the items in the main word pair more specifically by identifying *how* the roof functions in relation to the house: "A ROOF is the outside top covering of a HOUSE." When we test the analogy relationship of choice (C), we find that the choice is incorrect, because a lid is not the outside top covering of a container—it *is* the top. Choice (E) is also incorrect, because the apex is not the outside top covering of a triangle, but it is the top angle of the triangle. The correct choice is (D), because hair is the outside top covering of the head.

    Now try the following analogy that presents a whole-to-part relationship:

Example

FACULTY : TEACHER ::

(A)   dollar : cent
(B)   meter : centimeter
(C)   house : door
(D)   week : day
(E)   team : player

Approach: Begin by creating a sentence that expresses the relationship between the items in the main word pair. A "faculty" is defined as a "body of all the teachers in a school, college, or university," and so the relationship expressed in the main word pair is *whole to part*. Examine the answer choices and you will see that all the choices contain comparisons between a whole and one of its parts. Thus, to create only a simple whole-to-part comparison sentence for the main word pair would not adequately narrow the relationship, because all the answer pairs would fit:

A TEACHER is part of a FACULTY.

A *cent* is part of a *dollar*.

A *centimeter* is part of a *meter*.

A *door* is part of a *house*.

A *day* is part of a *week*.

A *player* is part of a *team*.

The similarity of these phrases requires that we make the main-word-pair relationship sentence more specific, to phrase it as follows: "A TEACHER is one member of a FACULTY." Now, if we do that and substitute the answer choices in this sentence, we find that only one of the answer-choice relationships matches the relationship of the main word pair: One cent is *not* one member of a dollar; a centimeter is *not* one member of a meter; a door is *not* one member of a house; a day is *not* one member of a week. What we do find is that a player *is* one member of a team.

Relating the Container to Something Contained

Analogies that relate containers to the items that they contain are a lot harder to work with than you might imagine, because we often become accustomed to placing items into or assigning items to containers that are not really suited for them. Consider the following: dessert : dish. How might you phrase a relationship sentence? Would you consider the relationship one of a *container* related to *something that it might contain*? If so, you might say: "Dessert is served in a dish"— and you would be incorrect, because dessert is served *on* a dish but *in* a bowl. Consider the following:

Example

GRANARY : CORN ::

(A) ocean : fish
(B) water : droplet
(C) dish : dessert
(D) gemstone : jewelry
(E) vault : money

Approach: Begin by creating a sentence that expresses a meaningful and clear relationship between the items in the main word pair. If you do not know the meaning of the term "granary," it is a structure in which grain is stored. Thus, the main-word-pair relationship sentence might be: "A GRANARY is used to store CORN." Test each of the answer choices to see which exhibit a similar relationship, and be careful to apply the terms in the order in which they appear in the answer choices. Applying the relationship sentence, you will find that choices (A), (B), (C), and (D) are incorrect. An ocean is not used to store fish—fish live in an ocean. Water is not used to store a droplet—water is made up of droplets. A dish is not used to store a dessert—dessert is served on a dish. A gemstone is not stored in jewelry—a gemstone may be used in making jewelry. The only correct answer choice is (E), because a vault is used to store money.

ANOTHER EXAMPLE

Let's try another example of this type of relationship to sharpen your perception.

Example

DOCUMENTS : BRIEFCASE::

(A) letters : mailbox
(B) money : wallet
(C) fruit : supermarket
(D) books : library
(E) articles : magazine

Approach: A quick look at the main word pair and the answer choices shows that all relate items and the places in which they normally might be found. You will find documents in a briefcase, letters in a mailbox, money in a wallet, fruit in a supermarket, books in a library, and articles in a magazine. Thus, you already know that constructing a sentence that simply states that the items are found within the larger item will be inadequate. Examine the main word pair more closely to determine how you can state the relationship between the documents and the briefcase in a more specific manner. Are documents stored in a briefcase? Or is a briefcase used to *transport* or *carry* documents? This seems to be a more likely specific relationship. Now try the word pairs from the answer choices. Is a mailbox used to transport letters? No. Is a wallet used to transport money? Yes. Is a supermarket used to transport fruit? No. Is a library used to transport books? No. Is a magazine used to transport articles? No. Thus, choices (A), (C), (D), and (E) are incorrect, because the word pairs in these answer choices do not have the same relationship as do those in the main word pair. Only choice (B) is correct.

Relating a General Term to a More Specific Term

In Chapter 9, you reviewed the analogy relationship in which you related an object to a specific condition or association, and you were asked to practice using more specific descriptive words when you write or speak. Analogies that require you to relate a general term to more specific terms call upon the same skills. When you speak—rather than refer in general to books, instruments, or professions—name the book, instrument, or profession specifically. The more that you practice expressing yourself in specific language, the more proficient you will become in dealing with all analogy relationships—and especially with the analogy relationships that ask you to relate the general term to the more specific.

Example
VOICE : SOPRANO::

- (A) guitar : string
- (B) band : violin
- (C) movie : review
- (D) instrument : trumpet
- (E) ballet : dance

Approach: Begin by devising a meaningful and clear relationship sentence: "A SOPRANO is a specific type of VOICE." When you test the answer word pairs, you immediately identify choices (A), (B), and (C) as incorrect. Choice (A) is incorrect; because a string is part of a guitar. In choice (B), a violin is a part of a band, but it is not a *type* of band. Choice (C) offers no relationship, and in choice (E) the strong relationship between the two words is invalid as an answer, because the terms are reversed. Thus, choice (D) is correct, because a trumpet is a type of instrument.

ANOTHER EXAMPLE

The *general-to-specific* analogy type that appears on the SAT also includes actions and ideas that may refer to the same basic activity or thinking and yet differ in that one is a general term and the other is specific. You have already found in your practice with analogies that reflect degree-of-intensity relationships in Chapter 8 that they are very similar to general-to-specific analogy relationships, and so the example below will appear familiar.

Example

PILFER : STEAL ::

(A) reduce : enlarge

(B) bicker : argue

(C) humiliate : embarrass

(D) run : jump

(E) walk : stumble

Approach: Create a meaningful and clear relationship between the items in the main word pair: "To PILFER is to STEAL on a small scale." When you try out the answer choices in this sentence, you find that choices (A), (D), and (E) exhibit no relationship between the words in the pairs. To reduce is not to enlarge on a small scale, to run is not to jump on a small scale, and to walk is not to stumble on a small scale. Choice (C) is also incorrect, because the terms are reversed. Only choice (B) is correct, because to bicker is to argue on a small scale.

Your review of analogies is almost at an end. We have covered most of the analogy types in the three chapters to this point, but you still have to tackle the special analogy challenges that result when you relate people to what they do or act upon and the purpose, quality, and places with which they are associated. Let's move on.

Chapter 11

Analogies

People and Professions

Analogies that describe people or that relate them to characteristics, places, professions, or purposes are the best-liked analogy types among many students, who claim that these analogies seem to present more "real" relationships than those testing the ability to relate abstract nouns or qualities. You will also find that they may be easier to understand from the viewpoint of vocabulary, because they usually include fairly easy, everyday words—or, at least, many more familiar words that do appear in business publications and newspapers in articles that deal with people and professions.

The trick in mastering this type of analogy lies more in developing the ability to accurately identify the relationships rather than in understanding the vocabulary used to describe those relationships. Don't be fooled, however, into thinking that vocabulary is of little importance in correctly identifying the relationship in analogies related to people—that would be a mistake. You should still expect to run into unfamiliar terms and associations, and some of us who might be a little more theoretical in our thinking and less familiar with a wide range of occupations will find these *more* rather than less difficult. This should be no surprise, because you have already seen in the preceding four chapters of analogy review that some types appeal more to your strengths than others and that you actually find certain types of analogy relationships easier to understand.

Relating People and Their Qualities

Our many experiences with people often color the way in which we react to the terms that we and others use to describe the nature and purpose of their roles, professions, and goals. These reactions are the associations with various words that have accumulated over time, and they form the *connotations* that we attach to words. As you recall from reviewing word connotation and denotation when working with sentence-completion skills in Chapter 3, even the most concrete terms may have personal associations for us—and those personal associations may interfere with our ability to clearly identify analogy relationships. This is especially true of analogies that relate people to the qualities expected to be associated with their roles, and such associations also influence the way in which we characterize professions. Because of this influence, you will have to train yourself to eliminate all personal associations—as you should in responding to all analogy relationships.

Example

TRAITOR : LOYAL ::

(A)   miser : greedy

(B)   physician : kind

(C)   philanthropist : stingy

(D)   soldier : brave

(E)   actor : handsome

Approach: Begin by identifying the relationship in the main word pair. The relationship is between a noun and an adjective. The quality described by the adjective is the *opposite* of the quality usually associated with this specific noun, and so it shows a *lack* of the usually associated quality.

By definition, a "traitor" is someone who is *"dis*loyal," *not* someone who is loyal, as the analogy relationship states. Thus, you must look for an answer choice that contains this same opposite relationship. The answer choices do not offer you any means of quickly eliminating one or more of them, because the parts of speech in all five are in the same order as the main word pair: noun : adjective. Therefore, you must create a meaningful and clear relationship sentence using the main word pair: "A TRAITOR is someone who is by definition not LOYAL." Now, insert the answer choices and you find that choices (B), (D), and (E) can be eliminated because the adjectives are not strongly associated with the nouns. A physician is not necessarily either kind or not kind. A soldier may be brave, but not all are brave. An actor might be handsome, but many actors who are not handsome become successful as well. Choice (A) is also incorrect because by definition a miser is greedy, and so the description is correct but the relationship to the main word pair is not. Only choice (C) is correct, because a philanthropist is by definition generous, not stingy.

Relating People and Their Purposes

Analogies that relate people to their purposes actually describe relationships between people and the functions they perform or the roles they play. Such analogies may be of two types, and the main-analogy word pair may present one of the following: (1) a relationship between a person identified by a main activity or occupation and an associated action or purpose that is expressed in verb form *or* (2) a relationship between a person identified by a main activity or occupation and a noun that describes an associated action or purpose.

Example

SURGEON : OPERATE ::

(A) gambler : lose

(B) watchman : walk

(C) teacher : discipline

(D) play : musician

(E) scientist : investigate

Approach: Examine the relationship that appears in the main word pair and you find that the analogy is made between a noun that names a profession and a verb that accurately names an action essential to that profession. If you review the answer choices, not all present word pairs that clearly reflect the parts of speech appear in the main word pair, i.e., in choices (B), (C), and (D), walk, discipline, and play, may function as either nouns or verbs. This observation is just a reminder to look for homographs, as you learned in Chapter 5, and it will not affect the outcome of this analogy item because the main word pair contains two clearly identifiable parts of speech. Now, create a meaningful and clear relationship sentence using the main word pair: "The major purpose of a SURGEON is to OPERATE." Next, insert the answer choices and you find that you can immediately eliminate choice (D), because the terms are reversed. Choices (A), (B), and (C) are also incorrect choices. The major purpose of a gambler is not to lose, although gamblers do often lose. The major purpose of a watchman is not to walk, although a large part of the watchman's time is spent in walking. The major purpose of a teacher is not to discipline but to teach. Only choice (E) is correct, because the major purpose of a scientist is to investigate.

ANOTHER EXAMPLE

A second analogy form of this type relates two nouns in the main word pair to suggest the relationship between people and their functions or the roles that they play.

Example

LAWYERS: LITIGATION ::

(A) writer : relaxation
(B) magician : delusion
(C) swimmer : competition
(D) isolation : monk
(E) politician : conservation

Approach: Examine the relationship that appears in the main word pair and you find that the analogy is made between a noun that names a profession and another noun that accurately names an action essential to that profession. Create a meaningful and clear relationship sentence using the items in the main word pair: "A major activity of a LAWYER is to engage in LITIGATION." Now, insert the answer choices in the sentence and you find that choice (D) is obviously incorrect, because a monk may seek isolation but the terms are reversed. The relationships in choices (A), (C), and (E) are all possible activities of the professions named, but they are not the major activities and so they are incorrect, as well. One activity of a writer may be relaxation, but it is not the major activity. A swimmer may engage in competition, but not all swimmers do so. A politician may be a proponent of conservation, but it is not the main activity of politicians. The only correct choice is (B), because the main activity of a magician is delusion.

Relating People (or Subjects) to Places

This analogy type asks us to modify the subheading a little, because you may find that you are not just asked to relate a person in a profession to the place in which that profession is usually practiced. You might find that analogies will also include animals that you must relate to their correct habitats, i.e., bear : den, trout: stream, and so on.

In some tests, the items of this analogy type will limit a main word pair and its answer choices to only all human subjects or only all animal subjects. In other cases, the subjects are mixed. Whether the choices are separate or mixed, you should approach all types in the same manner.

Example

SCULPTOR : STUDIO ::

(A)   senator : elevator
(B)   driver : taxicab
(C)   pilot : airplane
(D)   judge : courtroom
(E)   astronomer : sky

Approach: Examine the relationship between the items in the main word pair and in the answer choices. You find that all pairs contain nouns related to each other. Now, create a meaningful and clear relationship sentence using the items in the main word pair: "A SCULPTOR works in a STUDIO." When you insert the answer choices into the sentence, you immediately find that choices (A) and (E) are incorrect. A senator may ride in an elevator but not necessarily work there. An astronomer studies the sky as an activity of his or her profession but does not work in the sky. Choices (B) and (C) present more of a challenge, because both the driver and the pilot are inside the taxicab and airplane, respectively, while they work. We must modify the main-word-pair sentence to make it more specific: "The room in which a SCULPTOR works is a STUDIO." When we, once again, try out choices (B) and (C), we find that they no longer fit, because neither the taxicab nor the airplane is a room. Only choice (D) is correct, because the room in which the judge works is the courtroom.

ANOTHER EXAMPLE—ANIMALS AND THEIR HABITATS

You will also encounter analogies that require you to associate an animal subject with a specific place or habitat.

Example

BIRD : CAGE::

(A)   hutch : rabbit
(B)   elephant : zoo
(C)   monkey : tree

(D) lion : den
(E) trout : stream

Approach: Examine the main word pair and the answer choices and you find that all items contain nouns related to nouns, an animal to a place in which it lives. Create a meaningful and clear sentence using the items in the main word pair: "A BIRD lives in a CAGE." If you substitute the items from the answer choices, you find that the terms in choice (A) are reversed, and so you can eliminate that choice. The remaining choices are still possibilities, because the animals named all may live in the places named. You must, therefore, make the main-word-pair relationship sentence more specific by specifying what makes the relationship between the bird and the cage strong: "A BIRD in captivity lives in a CAGE." This statement is suitably specific, because not all birds live in cages. Birds in the wild do not. When you insert the answer choices in this sentence, you find that the relationships of the items in choices (C), (D), and (E) do not match the relationship between the items of the main word pair, because they imply freedom, not incarceration. A monkey in captivity does not live in a tree. A lion in captivity does not live in a den. A trout in captivity does not live in a stream. Thus, the only correct choice is (B), because an elephant in captivity does live in a zoo.

You have now reviewed the range of sentence-completion questions and analogy relationships that appear on the SAT verbal section. The skills that you have developed will be very useful in understanding the reading passages that follow and in helping you to understand what the questions ask of you. Reading comprehension sections call upon all these skills—and require further that you concentrate for longer periods of time than are required by the sentence-completion items and analogies. Armed with what you have learned to this point, you are ready to tackle the final type of verbal assessment that appears on the SAT. Start now.

Chapter 12

Reading Comprehension

Strategies and Main Ideas

One-half of the verbal items on the SAT are reading comprehension questions. Think about that for a moment. Here's something else to ponder—everything that you have practiced to this point is necessary for success with the reading comprehension passages. So if you have skipped any of the first eleven chapters, go back and review.

Are you ready to work? Good. Let's go.

Developing Your Strategies

You cannot develop your strategies for success until you know the terrain, so let's review the format of the reading comprehension questions. As you already know, you will face seven sections on the SAT—three verbal and four mathematics *or* four verbal and three mathematics, but only three of each will actually count—and all three verbal sections contain either one long reading passage or two brief passages in a dual-passage section. Most students are so stressed while responding to the test questions that they do not even notice that the passages are drawn from different subject areas: *humanities, social sciences, natural science,* and *literature* (either a fiction or a nonfiction narrative). Although you do not have a choice and you do have to respond to all the passages, knowing that the subject areas are varied should calm some of your concerns. Why? Each of us has special areas of interest, and we tend to respond better to readings that fall within those areas of interest. So if you are more interested in natural science than in humanities, you will probably consider the passage on a subject in science to be more interesting and, thus, easier to understand and respond to. At the same time, you should probably go on full alert when approaching the humanities selection, because you already know that you will not become as involved in the material. As a result, responding to the comprehension questions will be more difficult.

Reading and Understanding the Questions

Once you have identified the type of passage to which you are responding, you should also identify the types of questions asked about the passage. Some might disagree, but to take the most complete approach to reading comprehension passages, you should review the questions before reading the passage and identify the types of questions you will have to answer. Will they be specific or general? Stated or implied? Straightforward or phrased in vague terms? If a question asks you to locate information about a specific date, jot the date in the margin of the passage and then circle each time that you come to it in your reading. Do the same with specific names or incidents. You will save time and aggravation by doing so.

What types of questions appear in the reading comprehension sections of the SAT verbal section? Reading comprehension questions fall into five categories:

1. *Main idea* or *generalization* questions that ask you to identify the main idea of a passage, either directly or by asking that you provide a title or a summary or that you draw a generalization from the information
2. *Text details* questions that ask you to read the lines of the passage and then provide specific facts and details that appear in the passage
3. *Inference* questions that ask you to read *between* the lines of the passage and to provide answers that are suggested by the passage and the author
4. *Author's attitude* questions that ask you to identify the tone or mood created in the passage by the author
5. *Language assessment* questions that ask you to identify the ways in which specific words or phrases are used in the passage, similar to the sentence-completion items based on context clues

In this and the chapters that follow, you will learn how to determine specifically what information the questions ask and how to locate that information quickly.

How can you be certain of what the question asks? Most of the questions that appear in the SAT verbal sections follow specific patterns and use specific verbs that signal their intentions. Review Table 12-1 and memorize the typical question formats and verbs that alert you to the type of information asked by the questions.

Table 12-1 Typical Question Patterns

Question Type	Question Pattern and Verb
Main idea or generalization	"The main purpose of the passage is … ."
	"The passage is mainly (primarily) concerned with … ."
	"A good title for the passage is … ."
	"In the last sentence of the paragraph the word 'it' refers to … ."
	"The chief focus of the passage is on which of the following … ?
	"Which of the following best summarizes the content of the passage?"
Text details	"According to the author, the use of … ."
	"In the passage, _____ is used to _____ … ."
	"According to the passage, a _____ is _____ to _____ … ."
	"In the defense of _____, the author mentions all of the following EXCEPT … ."
	"The author refers to _____ as an example of … ."
	"The author cites _____ for their … ."
	"According to the passage, the following happens when … ."
Inference	"The passage suggests … ."
	"The passage implies that … ."
	"Based on the passage, one can infer … ."
	"One could easily see that … ."

	"Which of the following statements is the author of the passage LEAST/MOST likely to agree with?"
Author's Attitude	"The author's tone is best described as ... ."
	"Which of the following BEST describes the author's attitude toward the subject of the passage?"
	"It may be assumed that the author of this passage considers ... ."
	"The writer would probably classify the expression _____ as ... ."
Language Assessment	"The word _____ in line 16 is meant to suggest ... ."
	"The phrase _____ in the first paragraph means ... ."
	"The author uses the phrase _____ in lines 29–30 to mean ... ."
	"The best example of figurative language is ... ."

Before you tackle a reading comprehension passage, review the questions that follow it and label each question according to type. Then focus your attention on obtaining the information that the questions require. In all cases, answer the questions based only on the information found within the passage.

Consider the following example: You might be confronted with a reading passage from the natural sciences on the topic of mollusks. Perhaps that was your favorite area of study in biology and you may have a very strong knowledge of the topic. The passage might not go into as much depth as you can, but a question that asks you to supply an answer *according to the information given in the passage* might offer very specific and accurate information as one of the answer choices. The information in the answer choice may not appear in the passage, but you know that item containing the specific information is the best choice. Of course, you are tempted to select the answer that is correct and most specific. *Do not do so!* If you are asked to respond "according to the passage," then stick to the information found *only* in the passage, because any other response raises questions about your reading comprehension skills—and the answer will be wrong.

Reading the Passages Effectively

Take a box of sharpened pencils to the test site, and use your pencils liberally as you read the reading comprehension passages. As you begin to read, try to locate the thesis or main-idea statement in the opening paragraph of the passage and underline it. Then underline and place asterisks next to specific information that relates to the thesis statement in the supporting paragraphs. Such information might include specific names, dates, and facts that might be details called for in the text detail questions.

Circle *relationship words* and *phrases* in the passage. Such words and phrases enhance meaning because they provide a context by relating two sentences or parts of the same sentence in ways to show the *similarity, contrast, cause and effect,* and *time and sequence,* and also *to illustrate a point.* Table 12-2 presents some typical relationship words and phrases. You studied the use of many of the words and phrases that you will see in the table when you worked with sentence completions in Chapter 2.

Table 12-2   Helpful Relationship Words and Phrases

Function	Relationship Words and Phrases
To exhibit *similarity*	additionally, besides, furthermore, in fact, in the same way, likewise, moreover, similarly
To exhibit *contrast*	although, but, even so, however, in contrast, in spite of, instead, nevertheless, on the contrary, on the other hand, rather, still, yet
To exhibit *cause and effect*	accordingly, as a result, because, consequently, for, inevitably, since, so, so that, therefore
To exhibit *time and sequence*	afterward, at the same time, at this point, by now, earlier, eventually, finally, first, immediately, later, meanwhile, next, now, previously, simultaneously, subsequently, that day, the day before, the next day, then, thereafter, until, when, while
To illustrate a point	another, for example, for instance, for one thing, mainly, to begin with

Determining the Main Idea of the Passage

As you read, try to formulate a general summary statement that explains for you the mood or the tone of the passage, as well as a general summary statement that explains the purpose of the passage. You should also make notes in the margin of the passage consisting of phrases or statements that state what the facts in the passage seem to imply. Your notes may contain key words that might also appear in a question asking you to select the "best title" for the passage. Be on the alert for summary statements in the passage that will do the work of signaling the main idea: "all in all," "finally," "in conclusion," "in short," "so," "therefore," "thus."

If you find that some of the sentences do not seem to make sense, place a checkmark or other mark next to them for your further review, because you will not be able to express fully the meaning of the passage if you do not understand all that you have read. You should also attempt to understand the meanings of all words in the passage in order to understand the entire passage. Even if some of the vocabulary is difficult, use the skills that you developed in preparing for the sentence completions to use word parts (prefix, root, or suffix) or context clues to come close to the meaning of the words.

Example

It would be the last of her many weary journeys with her young and doubtless often fretful family. Her little space of comedy was about to end in a tragedy, one of many which pursued her son Edgar through the remainder of his astonishing life. As she drove through the arch of the wagon yard of the old Indian Queen Tavern and ensconced herself in the rooms behind and over the milliner shop of the good Mrs. Phillips, she entered upon the last scene of the last act. Perhaps in her heart she knew it, for she had already been very ill and must have been, from the nature of the events which were soon to follow, in a consumptive condition, and a low state of health.

(127 words)

1. Which of the following titles best summarizes the content of the passage?
   (A) One Woman's Sad Life
   (B) A History of Defeat
   (C) No Rest for the Weary
   (D) A Mother's Final Illness
   (E) The Results of Alcoholism

2. The passage as a whole principally deals with the
   (A) death of an alcoholic mother
   (B) final days of a woman worn out by life's cares
   (C) view of life as a drama on stage
   (D) care of seriously ill people
   (E) abuse of a child by his mother

Approach: Questions that ask you to select the best title for a passage are really variations on the main-idea question. Therefore, the title that you choose should reflect the entire selection—not merely one idea contained within the selection. The only difference is in the way that you must think of the response, which is not in the usual form of a statement. Instead, as you read the passage, think of a headline that might characterize the material. Question 1 offers five possible titles, all related in some way to the passage. Choices (C) and (E) take their cues from information provided in the passage, but they distort the information. Although the woman is portrayed as worn out by life, the passage simply relates that she is headed for a new place to live, but it does not offer a judgment on whether or not she will find rest at her new home, making choice (C) incorrect. The error in choice (E) is more glaring, because the passage does not indicate the woman was ill because she was an alcoholic, but rather that she had consumption (tuberculosis). The reader should not be misled by the sole mention of the Indian Queen Tavern, which is only located near where the woman will live and is not where she is headed. Choices (A) and (B) are both suggested by the passage, but we learn of only a small part of the woman's life, not the entirety that choices (A) and (B) suggest. Choice (D) becomes our best choice, because the woman in the passage is a mother (note the mention of "her son Edgar") and the passage states that she had been very ill and she has "entered upon the last scene of the last act." Choices (C) and (E) are incorrect because they require that the reader infer too much from the information given, and the question asks that you identify what the passage "principally deals with," not what it suggests.

Handle question 2 in the same way that you handle the title question, because both require that you understand the main idea of the passage. Choices (A) and (C) are incorrect, because they contain distortions based on isolated information contained in the passage. The fact that the woman is driving through the arch of the wagon yard of the old Indian Queen Tavern does not suggest that the woman is an alcoholic. Neither do the mentions that "her little space of comedy was about to end in a tragedy" and that she has "entered upon the last scene of the last act" dominate the passage. Choices (D) and (E) are incorrect because they require that the reader infer too much from the information given, and the question asks that you identify what the passage "principally deals with," not what it suggests. Choice (B) is correct because it is the most specific and best brings together the information contained in the passage.

Single Passage or Dual (Paired) Passages?

All the preceding strategies and hints will strengthen your reading of and responding to the single or paired passages. Both types of reading passage sections require understanding of the content and questions, and both contain the same relationship words and question types. What differs is the structure. As you read each passage, keep in mind that the selections are carefully chosen to make similar or contrasting points about one subject, and so aim to identify if the two approaches agree or disagree or if one provides an enhancement of the information found in the other.

The dual-passage (paired-passage) reading comprehension section contains two passages, 350 to 400 words each, that deal with either similar or contrasting views of the same topic. Of the approximately thirteen questions that are asked in this section, about one-third of the questions are asked solely about the first passage, a second third are asked solely about the second passage, and the remaining questions (usually four) ask you to relate both passages. To answer the largest number of questions correctly, deal with only *one passage at a time*. Each passage contains fewer words than the single-passage readings, and so handling each passage separately will increase your number of correct responses. The following procedure makes working with the two passages more manageable:

1. Review the questions to separate those that are asked about the individual passages from those that are asked about the combined passages.
2. Read the questions related to the first passage. Then read the passage and underline and circle key information as you do in the longer passages.
3. Answer the questions for the first passage before proceeding to the second passage.
4. Read the second passage in the same way as you handled the first. Then respond to only those questions related to the second passage.
5. Read the questions that relate to both passages *and* review the questions and your responses to the individual passages. You will often find that the questions that relate to both passages are combinations of questions asked about the individual passages.

All of the reading comprehension strategies that you review in this and in the following chapters are important in dealing with the dual-passage (or paired-passage) questions of the SAT verbal section, and so we do not have to review examples for both the single and dual passages. What works for one works for both.

Chapter 13

Reading Passages

Questions That Ask for Text Details

Have you ever taken an open-book test? That is how most students describe the type of reading comprehension questions dealt with in this chapter—as an open-book test in which they have to locate details and facts in a reading passage. However, just as the open-book test in the classroom is usually more difficult than the alternative because more specific questions may be asked, reading passage questions that ask for text details are similarly challenging.

Strategies and Trigger Words for Finding Text Details

The answers to *text detail* questions can usually be found clearly in the passage, either stated openly or related closely to a clearly identifiable detail in the passage. But which details are important? As you probably know, not every detail is critical, and you can only determine which are critical by reading the questions—but *not the answer choices*—beforehand. Questions that look for text details are usually phrased in the following manner:

"According to the author, the use of … ."

"In the passage, _____ is used to _____ … ."

"According to the passage, a _____ is _____ to _____ … ."

"In the defense of _____, the author mentions all of the following EXCEPT … ."

"The author refers to _____ as an example of … ."

"The author cites _____ for their … ."

"According to the passage, the following happens when … ."

Keep your attention clearly on text detail questions when reading the passage, so that you will efficiently underline, circle, and star the information that they call for. If necessary to keep you on track, circle the numbers of text detail questions and place a "T" next to each before you begin. For an even more efficient approach, underline major words in the question to focus your attention on the key concepts that you should pursue.

Example

1 Both Darwin and John Stuart Mill recognized, by
2 inference at least, the fact that so-called "natural checks"—and
3 among them war—will operate if some sort of limitation is not
4 imposed. In his *Origin of Species,* Darwin says: "There is no
5 exception to the rule that every organic being naturally increases
6 at so high a rate, if not destroyed, that the earth would soon be
7 covered by the progeny of a single pair." Elsewhere he observes
8 that we do not permit helpless human beings to die off, but we
9 create philanthropies and charities, build asylums and hospitals
10 and keep the medical profession busy preserving those who could
11 not otherwise survive. John Stuart Mill, supporting the views of
12 Malthus, speaks to exactly the same effect in regard to the
13 multiplying power of organic beings, among them humanity. In
14 other words, let countries become overpopulated and war is
15 inevitable. It follows as daylight follows the sunrise.

(154 words)

1. According to the passage, to keep human beings from dying off, people do all of the following EXCEPT
   (A) create philanthropies
   (B) build hospitals
   (C) pass legislation
   (D) build asylums
   (E) create charities

2. In the passage, the author identifies one of the so-called "natural checks" on overpopulation as

(A) daylight
(B) the medical profession
(C) hospitals
(D) war
(E) organic beings

Approach: How should you approach the above questions? First, read the questions, but ignore the answer choices for now. Decide which questions ask you to provide text details, as opposed to those that ask you to determine the main idea, draw inferences, identify the author's influence, and assess the use of language. In those questions that ask for text details, underline the key words and specific phrases that you must locate when reading the passage. Decide what you are looking for—dates, names, financial facts? Then, read the passage with your pencil in hand to underline details that appear to reflect what you need.

Review the questions and you see that the structure and wording identify them as text detail questions. You are expected to work only with the material that appears in the passage, because question 1 directs that the answer be determined "according to the passage" and question 2 states "in the passage." Now, what are the key words or phrases in each question? Underline them or enclose them within brackets to remind you of your focus in each question.

(T) 1. According to the passage, [to keep human beings from dying off], people do all of the following EXCEPT
- (A) create philanthropies
- (B) build hospitals
- (C) pass legislation
- (D) build asylums
- (E) create charities

(T) 2. In the passage, the author identifies one of the so-called ["natural checks"] on overpopulation as
- (A) daylight
- (B) the medical profession
- (C) hospitals
- (D) war
- (E) organic beings

Now read the passage and underline words or phrases that seem to relate to words that you underlined or bracketed in the text detail questions.

Example

1 Both Darwin and John Stuart Mill recognized, by
2 inference at least, the fact that so-called <u>"natural checks"</u>—and
3 <u>among them war</u>—will operate if some sort of limitation is not
4 imposed. In his *Origin of Species,* Darwin says: "There is no
5 exception to the rule that every organic being naturally increases
6 at so high a rate, if not destroyed, that the earth would soon be
7 covered by the progeny of a single pair." Elsewhere he observes
8 that <u>we do not permit helpless human beings to die off,</u> but we
9 <u>create philanthropies and charities, build asylums and hospitals</u>
10 and keep the medical profession busy preserving those who could
11 not otherwise survive. John Stuart Mill, supporting the views of
12 Malthus, speaks to exactly the same effect in regard to the
13 multiplying power of organic beings, among them humanity. In
14 other words, <u>let countries become overpopulated and war is</u>
15 <u>inevitable.</u> It follows as daylight follows the sunrise.

(154 words)

After identifying specifically which text details the questions ask about and then reading the passage and underlining key ideas and phrases, return to the questions and examine each of the answer choices. Question 1 comes with two demands: (1) "According to the passage" means that the correct answer must appear in the passage and (2) "EXCEPT" requires that you identify the answer that contains information *not* true of the passage. Locate in the passage the phrase similar to the one that you underlined in the question, "to keep human beings from dying off." It appears in line 8: "we do not permit helpless human beings to die off." Examine choices (A), (B), (D), and (E) and you will find them mentioned explicitly in the passage in line 9. Nowhere in the passage does the author state that people pass legislation to "not permit human beings to die off." Thus, the correct answer is choice (C).

Question 2 asks you to find one of the "natural checks" on overpopulation, and so the information must appear in the passage. Follow the procedure from above and locate in the passage the phrase that you underlined in the question, "natural checks." It appears in line 2, and it is followed in line 3 by an example of one of these "natural checks"—"war." Answer choices (A), (B), (C), and (E) are all named in the passage, but only choice (D), "war," is identified in the passage as a "natural check." Thus, the correct answer is choice (D).

Finding Combined Details

A variation on the questions that require you to identify details found directly in the text is the kind of questions that seek a response that combines two or more details. To answer this type of question, you will follow the same basic procedure that you followed to find the single text detail. This time, however, you will have a little more text to read in the question, because you will be faced with five different details that must be assessed. Underline the key words in the statements before reading the passage, as before, and try to determine if the statements follow a trend of thought. Then, as with the single detail, read the passage and underline all key facts and phrases. When you return to the questions, read through all the statements carefully, noting the key words and phrases that you underlined. Place a line through the statements that contain details that you have not read in the passage. Read the remaining statements, and then look back at the passage to check if they reflect the details in the passage. Make certain that the statements you select as valid do not leave out any details.

Example

1 Child labor has proved harmful to mental development, even to
2 the extent of stunting children for life. Opportunities in evening
3 classes are not worth much, for the child is so tired after a hard
4 day's work that he grows drowsy over his books. He is cheated,
5 thus, not only out of a normal play life and normal physical
6 development, but also out of the opportunity to better his situation
7 through education.
8   The large majority of child laborers are engaged in agricultural
9 work. This does not mean the chores which farm children are

10 expected to perform, but hard work and long hours at picking
11 berries, harvesting cotton, or hoeing and weeding extensive beet
12 fields or onion fields. Many schools in rural sections have
13 sessions of only five or six months so that the children may be
14 available for work from the ploughing season to the harvesting
15 season. Whether the child works long hours on his father's farm
16 without pay or on a neighboring farm for wages, the result
17 on the child's welfare and the welfare of society is the same.

(197 words)

Question: Which of the following statements may be accurately derived from the selection?

I. Child laborers are able to better themselves through education.
II. Most child laborers work on farms.
III. Many rural schools are only in session for five or six months of the year.
IV. Child labor strengthens a child's mental development.
V. Working for wages is better for a child laborer than working on his father's farm for free.

(A) I only
(B) II and V
(C) II and III
(D) I, IV, and V
(E) II and V

Approach: Read through the statements before reading the passage. You see that statements I, IV, and V present positive outlooks for the child laborer, and statements II and III are neutral. Keep these distinctions in mind when you read through the passage and underline text details that refer to the statements. You learn almost immediately that statement I is incorrect, because lines 4 through 7 state that the child is "cheated ... out of the opportunity to better his situation through education." Once you know that statement I is not true, you can then eliminate any answer that contains I. So choices (A) and (D) are incorrect. Now read statement II and you find that this statement is true according to lines 8 and 9 in the passage. When you test statement III, you find that it is also true, based on lines 12 and 13. So a correct answer choice must contain both II and III. Only answer choice (C) contains both II and III, and so it seems to be the correct answer.

However, you should also test the remaining statements. Lines 1 and 2 of the passage contradict statement IV, and so answer (D) must be incorrect. Statement V is also not true, as the opposite appears in lines 15 through 17. Thus, the only correct answer is (C).

Use the strategies in this chapter to determine answers to all questions that require you to relate details from the text of a passage. Your next step is to learn how to answer reading comprehension questions that ask you to interpret. Let's get started.

Chapter 14

Reading Passages

Questions That Ask You to Draw Inferences

You are about to enter the world of drawing *inferences*, a world beyond mere text detail questions that ask you to read the lines and identify factual information. You will go beyond the facts, to read between the lines and to make judgments based on the information contained in a passage. Some of the questions ask you to select *inferences, interpretations,* and *comparisons* based on a single statement or single situation contained in the passage, while others ask you to consider the interaction of several facts. Your task is to select the most reasonable interpretation—and the one that most clearly reflects the facts in the passage.

Developing Your Strategies

To correctly interpret the importance of material that appears in the SAT reading comprehension passages, you have to build on the strategies reviewed in earlier chapters. Think of *drawing inferences, interpreting,* and *paraphrasing* as advanced training—but don't be intimidated by the task. Keep in mind that you are already an expert in drawing inferences.

Think of the many times each day that you hear a sound or see an action after which you make an assumption—an inference. When the judgment is made based on a careful consideration of the circumstances or facts, the inference is most likely to be accurate. When the judgment is based on unsound or inadequate observations, you draw inaccurate inferences.

Let's examine several everyday examples of facts and inferences before tackling the identification of inferences in the reading passages. Look at Table 14-1. The facts listed in the table lend themselves to many more interpretations (inferences) than appear in the table. Review the assumptions made about every fact and notice that each one requires more information to make it valid. Specific circumstances and additional information are necessary before a person can come to any of the listed conclusions with certainty. The same is true in drawing inferences and making interpretations for the SAT reading passages. You must consider a number of facts—not just one—in the passage for an inference or interpretation to be valid.

Table 14-1 Facts and Inferences

Fact	Possible Assumptions (Inferences)
A siren sounds.	• Police may be on a chase. • Firefighters are racing to a fire. • Schools in town are being closed. • Emergency services department is testing equipment.
A child sits on a bench in the mall and cries.	• The child has been accidentally separated from a parent. • The child has run away from home. • The child has been reprimanded by a parent and given a "time-out." • The child has escaped from a would-be kidnapper.
A friend fails to call at a promised time.	• The friend has forgotten. • The friend is angry about something. • Family obligations have interfered. • The telephone is not working.
The computer fails to respond when switched on.	• The operating system has crashed. • The electricity is out in the area. • The computer has become unplugged. • Interface cables have loosened.
A speaker fails to include a specific ethnic group in a speech that praises community cooperation.	• The speaker is biased against the group. • The speaker missed the group's name when referring to the notes. • The group has done nothing to help the community.

How do you know which questions ask you to identify an inference, interpretation, or paraphrase of material in the passage? As you found in working with text details, questions that draw inferences also contain specific words and phrases as clues:

"From the information in lines 23–24, we can assume … ."

"The details in the second paragraph *convey* which of the following?"

"The information in the second and third paragraphs *emphasizes* _____ … ."

"Which of the following does the passage *exemplify*?"

"The passage *implies* that _____ … ."

"The facts in paragraph 4 *indicate* … ."

"Based on the passage, one can *infer* … ."

"Which of the following may readers of the passage *presume*?"

"Given the conclusion, what does the author appear to *presuppose*?"

"To which of the following do the dates in the passage *refer*?"

"The quotations that appear in the passage *serve to* … ."

"The passage *suggests* … ."

"One *could easily see* that … ."

"The writer appears to *suppose* … ."

"The writer appears to *believe* … ."

"The passage *can best be described as* … ."

"*Judging by* the information in paragraph 7, the following is true … ."

"The information in the last two paragraphs is *used to illustrate* … ."

"The author of the passage is LEAST/MOST likely to agree with … ."

Making the Reasonable Choice

Knowing the phrases that signal an inference or interpretation question is the first step. Before choosing one answer over another, however, you must be able to support your choice with statements and facts found in the passage.

DEALING WITH THE INFERENCE QUESTION

The inference question asks you to make a judgment or an educated guess based on observations that appear in the passage. If the facts or statements of the passage do not support the possibility of an answer choice, then the inference is not correct. You should be able to clearly identify information in the passage—even underline specific facts and statements—that supports the assumption that you select. Consider the following passage that is taken from a handbook on social life published in the 1938.

Example

1 Courtship is a period when two personalities test
2 each other. A recent survey of a large number of
3 married couples shows that the group of couples who
4 had been engaged about a year had the largest percentage
5 of permanent marriages. For every period of courtship less
6 than a year, the percentage of permanent marriages sharply
7 decreased.

(63 words)

1. The passage implies that
    (A) people who are engaged are affectionate
    (B) courtship guarantees success in marriage
    (C) being engaged is like being married
    (D) the length of the period of courtship is very important to success in marriage
    (E) people who are engaged a year or longer will have a permanent marriage

2. The essential point being made about marriage is
    (A) that it is growing less popular
    (B) that it is permanent
    (C) that permanence depends upon the couple knowing each other well

(D) that everybody gets married
(E) that it is a very fragile institution

Approach: Begin by reading the questions and the answer choices before reading the passage, so that you will have an idea of the impressions that you are expected to gain. You will probably have to return to the passage as you test each inference choice, but knowing at the outset what you are looking for will save you time. At first glance, both questions seem to ask you to make the same inference, but you can see the clear differences once you read the answer choices of each question. The answer choices for question 1 are clearly related to the *connection between courtship and marriage,* while the answer choices for question 2 are clearly related to *marriage.*

Nowhere in the passage does the writer show any interest in assessing the personal interaction of the couple, engaged *or* married. Instead, the focus is on assessing the relationship between the length of the courtship period and the permanence of the marriage. In question 1, choice (A) is incorrect, because the passage makes no mention of affection. Choice (B) is also incorrect for two reasons. The word "guarantees" appears in the choice, but nowhere in the passage does a guarantee appear. Further, the passage does not speak of "success" in marriage—only permanence. Choice (C) is also incorrect, because the passage does not equate being engaged with being married. One of the reasons that makes choice (B) incorrect also makes choice (E) an incorrect inference, because the passage does not say that longer engagements will result in a permanent marriage—only that a larger number of marriages that follow longer engagements are permanent. Only choice (D) is a reasonable inference, because it states the connection between the length of engagement and the observed percentage of permanent marriages without suggesting guarantees.

The focus is clearly stated in question 2, but the inference that you must make is more comprehensive than the inference that you made in question 1. You can immediately eliminate choices (A) and (D), because the passage does not provide any facts or statements to suggest that marriage is growing any more popular or less popular, nor does the passage deal with who marries or who does not marry. The inference in answer choice (B) is incorrect, because it directly contradicts the information in the passage, which provides a means of projecting how to increase the percentage of permanent marriages. The characterization of marriage as a fragile institution in choice (E) is unsupported by the passage, because the focus is not on assessing the state of marriage but on establishing a guideline for increasing its permanence. Only choice (C) may be inferred from the passage, and this is accomplished by combining the facts related to the marriage permanence rates for couples who had been engaged about a year (lines 2–5) and the reasons for the decrease in permanent marriages (lines 5–7).

DEALING WITH PARAPHRASE AND INTERPRETATION QUESTIONS

Questions that call for interpretation of material in a reading comprehension passage usually ask that you paraphrase the material, or to state it in another way. Interpretation questions might be asked in the following ways:

"Which of the following best expresses the meaning of _____?"

"Which is the best interpretation of the quotation by _____?"

"The title that best summarizes the content of the passage is _____ ... ."

"The best word to describe _____ is ... ."

"An excellent adjective to describe the _____ is ... ."

Before you select among answer choices, always return to the passage to locate and to underline the specific word or phrase that you are asked to interpret. Restate the material in your own words before looking at the answer choices to be certain that you actually understand the material that you interpreting. When you are satisfied that you have captured the intention of the original word or phrase, review the answer choices to find one that is close in meaning to your interpretation. You actually have to paraphrase material to locate the correct interpretation, but you will also find specific paraphrase questions in the reading comprehension section that ask you to place material into your own words. Because you are not summarizing but interpreting, make certain that your paraphrase says the same as the original—and with the same amount of detail. The paraphrase should be nearly as long as the original, and it should exhibit your comprehension both of the material and of what might be inferred from the material. The example below contains both interpretation and paraphrase questions.

Example

1 Few people today understand the impact that American
2 author Edgar Allan Poe (1809–1849) had on literature both
3 here and abroad. In his day, Poe wrote reviews and published

4 reams of material about the writers of his time, panning some
5 and praising others. To our detriment, much of the literary
6 criticism has become the fodder of scholars, material no longer
7 seen as current and now viewed as only fit to line the shelves
8 of an academic library or, if fragile, to be locked away in
9 manuscript form like precious jewels that would be lost
10 forever if displayed. Today's readers only know of Poe from
11 the movies that used his titles but which often mutilated
12 beyond recognition his plots until they became paper and
13 celluloid corpses of unidentifiable origin. They may also
14 know him from the horrors that pervade their nightmares and
15 the nightmare works of contemporary writers such as Stephen
16 King and Clive Barker, both of whom owe a great deal to the
17 master. The dark soul behind the smiling face, the dead who
18 refuse to remain in their coffins, the evil lurking in the hearts
19 of men—but rarely women—are Poe's calling cards. Would
20 others have discovered his nightmare landscape had Poe not
21 provided the map? Perhaps. No, more than "perhaps" because
22 his is the map of the human mind, the human heart, the human
23 soul—in all of its dark disgrace and with all of its fears. He
24 did not invent that darkness and fear. What he did was to
25 make us remember it exists.

(283 words)

1. Which of the following best expresses the meaning of the phrase "only fit to line the shelves of an academic library"?
   (A) Poe's literary criticism is not safe for the general reading public.
   (B) Poe's literary criticism is no better than blank shelf paper.
   (C) Poe's literary criticism is too valuable to be in town public libraries.
   (D) Poe's literary criticism is thought to not be of interest to anyone but scholars.
   (E) Very little of Poe's literary criticism survives.

2. Which of the following titles best summarizes the content of the passage?
   - (A) Poe's Heart of Darkness
   - (B) Poe: Architect of Horror
   - (C) Saving Poe's Criticism
   - (D) Poe: A Man of Rare Intellect
   - (E) Poe's Influence on Today's Writers

3. Poe should be viewed as an important American writer because
   - (A) he published a lot of material
   - (B) other writers cover the same topics that he did
   - (C) he influenced both American and European writers
   - (D) films were made from his work
   - (E) his work is locked in libraries

4. Which is the best interpretation of "They may … nightmares …" (lines 13–14)?
   - (A) People dream of Poe.
   - (B) Poe captured people's worst fears in his writing.
   - (C) Poe is studied in dream analysis.
   - (D) Anyone could have written Poe's works.
   - (E) Eating before you go to bed will give you nightmares.

Approach: Before you review the questions and the answer choices, identify the type of questions that face you. Questions 1 and 2 ask that you supply interpretations, while questions 3 and 4 require that you provide a paraphrase of specific information. To answer question 1, locate the phrase in the reading passage and underline or place brackets around the phrase to isolate it from the rest of the text. Do not look at the answer choices yet. First, restate the phrase in your own words, and make certain that your words accurately reflect the original. Now, match the phrase stated in your words to the answer choices. Choice (B) is incorrect, for it appears too harsh; the phrase does specify that the literary criticism is at least "fit" for an academic library. Choice (E) is also incorrect, because a concern regarding how much of the criticism survives is not included in the phrase. Choice (A) seems to have the wrong meaning altogether in its misinterpretation of the word "fit." Although choice (C) might appear on first glance to be a good possibility, it fails to reflect the original, because something that is "only fit" would not be considered "too valuable" for the public libraries. The correct choice is (D), which accurately interprets the limited contemporary appeal of Poe's literary criticism.

Question 2 asks you to interpret the entire passage in your selection of a suitable title for the material. This is the time to use the skills that you developed in Chapter 12 to determine the main idea and title of a passage. Read through the answer choices to locate those that focus only on one idea in the passage, and reject them as being unsuitable to provide a title for the entire passage. Keep in mind that you are asked to select the *best* choice among the five listed, but that choice might not necessarily be the title that you would have written for the passage. Choices (A), (C), and (E) are incorrect, because they all focus on limited areas of the passage. Choice (B) is a bit broader in range, but the passage discusses more than Poe's writing about horror, and so this choice is also incorrect. This leaves choice (D) as the best choice among those provided.

Questions 3 and 4 ask that you paraphrase material appearing in the reading passage, although only question 4 specifically states the material to be paraphrased. Your first task in approaching question 3 is to locate that part of the passage that makes a specific point of Poe's importance as a writer and to underline or place brackets around the relevant phrase(s) or sentence(s). The significant material appears at the beginning of the passage, especially in lines 1 through 3. Paraphrase the lines, capturing the meaning of the original as closely as possible. Now, match your statement to the answer choices. You can immediately eliminate choice (A), because merely publishing large quantities of writing does not make a person an "important American writer," unless some other influence is identified. Choices (D) and (E) are also incorrect, because both facts appear in the passage with negative associations. Choice (B) might be correct, because he could seem to have influenced other writers if they cover the same topics he did, but the assertion is not strong enough. The only correct answer is choice (C), in which Poe's importance as a writer is clearly stated.

Question 4 asks that you paraphrase only a *portion* of a sentence, but you do need to consider the *entire* sentence in order to accurately convey the mood and meaning of the phrase. Underline the sentence, which appears here: "They may also know him from the horrors that pervade their nightmares and the nightmare works of contemporary writers such as Stephen King and Clive Barker, both of whom owe a great deal to the master." While any number of inferences might be true, this not your task, and so you must identify those answer choices that are too broad or that fail to reflect the specific details contained in the phrase. Choices (D) and (E) are meaningless in regard to the phrase, and so you can reject them outright. Choice (C) speaks not of Poe's horrors, but it links to the concept of dreams and the analysis of those dreams, and so this answer choice is also incorrect. Choice (A) *seems* promising, but upon closer scrutiny we realize that the original phrase is focused upon the "horrors," not upon the man, and so this choice is also incorrect. The best choice is (B), which links the content of people's nightmares with the content of Poe's horror writing.

At this point, you have covered most of the question types that are asked about the reading passage on the SAT verbal section. Still ahead may be your biggest challenge—understanding the impact of the author in the passage.

Chapter 15

Reading Passages

Questions about the Author's Role

How does the author make an impact on a reading comprehension passage? More important to you—what do you have to know to answer questions that assess that impact?

To evaluate the author's role, you will have to draw upon every skill that you have developed to this point—those related to handling reading comprehension questions as well as the earlier skills reviewed to strengthen your abilities in completing sentences and dealing with analogies. Text details are not important, but inference is. In fact, you will probably recognize many of the questions that ask about the author's *purpose, attitude,* or *tone* from your work with inference. Although similar questions might be asked, the big difference is that the responses must be based on the perspective of the author of the passage and not upon what you—the reader—perceive to be the purpose or interpretation of a passage or a sentence within a passage.

The following sentences, which also appear in Table 12-1 in Chapter 12, provide a brief list of the many ways of phrasing questions regarding the author's impact on a passage.

> "The main purpose of the _____ in this passage is to _____."
>
> "The author's tone is best described as … ."
>
> "Which of the following BEST describes the author's attitude toward the subject of the passage?"
>
> "It may be assumed that the author of this passage considers … ."
>
> "The writer would probably classify the expression _____ as … ."

These and many more questions ask you to enter the mind of a stranger, the writer—whose name, gender, age, ethnic background, and life experiences remain unknown to you—and to explain what that stranger's purpose, attitude, and tone are in regard to a passage that you are reading for the first time. The task is challenging, but not impossible when you have the right tools.

Let's begin.

Determining the Author's Purpose

Answering questions regarding the author's purpose either in writing the entire passage or in including certain details or a portion of the passage should recall the steps that you took in Chapter 12 to identify the main idea of a passage or its purpose. The approach is very similar, for you have to carefully infer information in both instances. As you did earlier, you must read the question carefully to make certain that you understand if the question asks for your judgment about the writer's purpose for the entire passage or for only a portion of it. You will often find that purpose questions sometimes omit mention of the author, but common sense makes us realize that the purpose of including certain information or of writing in a given way about a subject is naturally the purpose of the author and not of any other entity. That is what makes dealing with this area of the author's role relatively easy—because you have already reviewed the skill. What this chapter adds is the awareness that the purpose of a passage may be stated as either that of the passage, as we reviewed in Chapter 12, or that of the author, our present focus.

Following are several of the many ways in which questions about the author's purpose might be phrased:

"The author includes _____ in order to ... ."

"Which of the following best describes the author's purpose in the passage?"

"For which of the following reasons does the author include statistical information?"

"The author includes quotations by _____ in order to ... ."

"Which of the following best describes the purpose of the passage?"

Example

1   A recent news report about the difficulties that airline
2   passengers face in delayed and cancelled flights motivated a
3   backlash among viewers who refused to agree with the
4   conclusions voiced in the report. One particular source of
5   anger was the tendency of the report to soften the statistics
6   regarding the waiting times at airports. As one frequent flyer
7   stated, "They can say what they want about one- or two-hour
8   delays, but what about those of us who have been stuck in
9   airports waiting six or more hours? Don't tell us that this is
10 unusual." An examination of airport records nationwide
11 shows that such major airports as Newark International have
12 had an only 50% on-time rate for the past two years. The
13 report is expected to provide new incentive to government
14 agencies to create controls that will improve airport efficiency.

(139 words)

1. The author includes a quotation by a "frequent flyer" in order to
   (A) add a filler to an otherwise short article
   (B) point out the outrage of airline passengers
   (C) add news interest to the article
   (D) add human interest to the article
   (E) stir up trouble

2. Which of the following best describes the author's primary purpose in the passage?
   (A) to gain free airline tickets
   (B) to strengthen support for government intervention
   (C) to increase airline business
   (D) to criticize the news report
   (E) to expose the continued inefficiency of the airline industry

Approach: Review all the answer choices, and then locate the quotation in the article to see where it appears. Is the quotation simply slipped into the article without any strong relationship to surrounding sentences, or does it appear to provide specific support for the opinions expressed in the article? You can eliminate choices (A) and (E), because the quotation is integral to the argument made in the article, not simply placed there to add bulk or excitement. The quotation does not add "news interest" to the article, and so choice (C) is also incorrect. You are left with two choices, both of which might be a logical answer, but you must select the most likely answer. Although incorrect, choice (D) is a good possibility, because the quotation does add human interest to the article. The correct answer is choice (B), because the quotation is the expression of continued outrage by airline passengers, and this answer is more specific.

The key word in question 2 is "primary," and you should evaluate the answer choices with this word clearly in mind. After reviewing the answer choices, you can immediately eliminate choices (A) and (C), because the negative nature of the passage will not win the writer any favor (nor "free airline tickets") with the airlines, nor will it encourage increased business. Choice (D), "to criticize the news report," may be implied by the mention in lines 5 and 6 that the news report seemed to soften its criticism of the airlines, but the writer does not maintain this criticism throughout. Further, while one effect of the article may be "to strengthen support for government intervention," choice (B), it is not the main emphasis. The only correct choice is (E), because the material that the article adds to the news report *does* "expose the continued inefficiency of the airline industry."

Determining the Author's Attitude

Questions that ask you to identify the author's attitude are really asking you to put yourself in the author's place and to express the author's feelings toward a specific someone or something. For this reason, you should read each question very carefully to identify the specific person or object accurately, and then locate it in the passage after reading the entire passage to gain an accurate feeling for the author's views. The attitudes may range from admiration to disdain, as well as all the levels in between. The answer choices may also provide very specific attitudes that reflect the given passage, and you might be asked to select among such terms as "cold objectivity," "veiled disdain," or "reluctant admiration."

Following are several of the many ways in which questions about the author's attitude might be phrased:

"The author's attitude toward _____ is primarily one of ... ."

"Which of the following best expresses the author's attitude toward _____?"

"The use of the phrase _____ in lines 23–24 expresses the author's attitude toward _____ as ... ."

"Readers can infer from the passage that the author's attitude toward _____ is ... ."

As you have noticed, questions that ask you to identify the author's attitude about someone or something always contain the word "attitude" clearly stated.

Example

1 Few creatures capture our attention as does the panda bear,
2 the black-and-white living stuffed animal that is native to
3 China. Sadly, this creature has not reproduced frequently in
4 captivity, which has led to an exceedingly high interest among
5 zoologists in the mating habits of the panda. Every panda
6 birth in the United States has become a media event,
7 because we seem to have made it our mission to
8 increase the number of pandas worldwide and to return them
9 to their former strengths in number. Nature, however, has
10 played an almost cruel joke on us, because the interest in
11 panda reproduction is not shared by the pandas themselves.
12 As a recent scientific study has found, pandas are significantly
13 more interested in eating than in mating.

(141 words)

1. Which of the following best expresses the author's attitude toward the U.S. interest in panda mating habits?
   (A) clear distaste
   (B) disbelief
   (C) mild amusement

(D) cold objectivity

(E) clear amazement

2. The use of the phrase "living stuffed animal" in line 2 expresses the author's attitude toward the pandas as

(A) mild condescension

(B) nostalgia

(C) admiring support

(D) growing anger

(E) detached affection

Approach: Read question 1 carefully. Then go back to the passage to locate the lines that deal with the panda mating habits to specifically address the author's attitude toward them. The language of the passage includes the word "Sadly" to show that the author sympathizes with rather than feels hostile toward the lessening numbers of pandas worldwide, and so choices (A) and (D) are incorrect. Further, while the author seems to offer the mild rebuke that panda births have become media events, nowhere is surprise expressed about the attention to the pandas, and so choices (B) and (E) are also eliminated. The only correct choice is (C), not only through the process of elimination, but because the author relates near the end of the article the ironic observation that the pandas are disinterested parties in the mating habits that obsess zoologists.

Before responding to question 2, refer to the passage to locate the context of the phrase, which seems to be used in an affectionate manner to describe these giant creatures. You can immediately eliminate choices (A) and (D), because the author's use of the term is neither condescending nor a sign of anger. Further, the term does not refer to any sense of personal loss, and so choice (B) is incorrect. Although using a term that exhibits the benign nature of the creatures, "living stuffed animal," is positive, it is not necessarily supportive, and so choice (C) is incorrect, as well. The only correct choice is (E), which makes an unsentimental reference to stuffed animals usually beloved by children.

Determining the Author's Tone

The reading comprehension passages on the SAT focus primarily on presenting information, and so they are usually neutral in *tone*. You will, however, occasionally find a passage that clearly reflects an author's feelings, and you must read between the lines to identify the tone. Unlike the author's attitude, which is directed at a specific someone or something, tone is the overall impression that the writer conveys through a careful use of association-laden words. You have to read the entire passage to accurately identify the tone, which may be described by a wide range of adjectives ("objective," "reflective," "indifferent," "ironic," "argumentative," "sensational," and others) and nouns ("anxiety," "resignation," "sarcasm," "self-pity," "indifference," "mistrust," and others).

Following are several ways in which questions about tone may be expressed:

"The tone of the selection as a whole can best be described as _____."

"Which of the following lines can best be described as _____?"

"The tone of the title is intended to be _____."

Rather than view another passage, let's see how we might identify tone in a passage for which we have already identified the author's attitude toward various items.

Example

1 Few creatures capture our attention as does the panda bear,
2 the black-and-white living stuffed animal that is native to
3 China. Sadly, this creature has not reproduced frequently in
4 captivity, which has led to an exceedingly high interest among
5 zoologists in the mating habits of the panda. Every panda
6 birth in the United States has become a media event,
7 because we seem to have made it our mission to
8 increase the number of pandas worldwide and to return them
9 to their former strengths in number. Nature, however, has
10 played an almost cruel joke on us, because the interest in
11 panda reproduction is not shared by the pandas themselves.
12 As a recent scientific study has found, pandas are significantly
13 more interested in eating than in mating.

(141 words)

1. The tone of the passage as a whole can best be described as
   - (A) sarcastic
   - (B) sympathetic
   - (C) inquisitive
   - (D) relieved
   - (E) indifferent

2. Which of the following lines can best be described as *ironic*?
   - (A) 1–2
   - (B) 3–4
   - (C) 5–6
   - (D) 7–8
   - (E) 12–13

Approach: Read the answer choices for question 1, and then read the passage carefully to gain a feeling for the author's view of the subject. The writer takes a positive view of the topic, and so choices (A) and (E) are incorrect. The author is not questioning in regard to the topic, and so choice (C) is also eliminated. No solution to a problem occurs in the course of the passage, and so choice (D) is also incorrect. Through the process of elimination, the best choice is (B), "sympathetic."

To determine the author's tone in a specific area of the passage, carefully read the entire passage once again to understand the *overall tone* of the passage. From the rest of the passage, you realize that the writer uses a sympathetic tone overall, with most of the statements presented in a straightforward manner. Only lines 12–13, choice (E), are "ironic."

You have reviewed and practiced how to handle most of the difficult questions in the reading comprehension sections of the SAT. Only one section remains for you to conquer—the language techniques of the reading passages.

Chapter 16

Reading Passages

Assessing the Language

You may be tempted to skip most of this brief chapter, because you have already worked with context clues in Chapter 2 and with connotation and figurative language in Chapter 3. Resist the temptation to skip any part of the chapter, and, instead, turn your attention to sharpening these skills in reading comprehension passages. The basic skills required may be the same, but the context of the reading passage imposes slightly different constraints on your choices.

Identifying Diction and Figurative Language

Questions that ask you to identify the meaning and use of words in the context of reading comprehension passages require that you identify what a word means when it is used in a specific way in the given passage. Although you must put to use the skills that you studied in Chapter 2, in which you learned to determine word meaning in a sentence by such context techniques as pairing, direct explanation, comparison, contrast, sequence, and function words, you must also remember that words acquire special and additional meanings in a passage. The meaning of a word in a reading passage is dependent on its context not only in a specific sentence, but in the whole passage. Thus you must also read the entire passage since surrounding sentences also impact on the way in which a word is used.

Questions that ask you to evaluate the way in which the author of a passage uses specific words may be phrased in the following ways:

"The word _____ as used in line _____ is meant to suggest ... ."

"The author uses the word _____ throughout the passage to describe ... ."

"The word _____ as used in line _____ means ... ."

Understanding how words are used figuratively in a reading passage also requires that you recall the skills that you developed in Chapter 3, in which you used figurative language to attack sentence-completion questions. When you are asked to give the meaning of a metaphor or simile in a reading passage, you must first find the specific expression in the passage and then read both the entire sentence in which the word appears and the surrounding sentences.

Only one question format is used to ask you to identify the way in which the author uses a figurative expression: "The author uses the phrase _____ to describe ... ." Here is the passage about Poe again, with certain words and expressions italicized.

Example

1 Few people today understand the impact that American
2 author Edgar Allan Poe (1809–1849) had on literature both
3 here and abroad. In his day, Poe wrote reviews and published
4 *reams* of material about the writers of his time, *panning* some
5 and praising others. To our detriment, much of the literary
6 criticism has become the fodder of scholars, material no longer
7 seen as current and now viewed as only fit to line the shelves
8 of an academic library or, if fragile, to be locked away in
9 manuscript form like precious jewels that would be lost
10 forever if displayed. Today's readers only know of Poe from
11 the movies that used his titles but which often mutilated
12 beyond recognition his plots until they became
13 *celluloid corpses* of unidentifiable origin. They may also
14 know him from the horrors that pervade their nightmares and
15 the nightmare works of contemporary writers such as Stephen
16 King and Clive Barker, both of whom owe a great deal to the
17 master. The dark soul behind the smiling face, the dead who
18 refuse to remain in their coffins, the evil lurking in the hearts

19 of men—but rarely women—are Poe's *calling cards*. Would
20 others have discovered his nightmare landscape had Poe not
21 provided the map? Perhaps. No, more than "perhaps" because
22 his is the map of the human mind, the human heart, the human
23 soul—in all of its dark disgrace and with all of its fears. He
24 did not invent that darkness and fear. What he did was to
25 make us remember it exists.

(283 words)

1. The word "reams" in line 4 is meant to suggest
    (A) packages of paper
    (B) large amounts
    (C) numerous pages
    (D) unknown amounts
    (E) sheets

2. The word "panning" in line 4 means
    (A) ignoring
    (B) criticizing severely
    (C) writing about
    (D) thinking of
    (E) glorifying

3. The author uses the phrase "celluloid corpses" in line 13 to mean
    (A) mannequins
    (B) plastic bags
    (C) people
    (D) movies
    (E) books

4. "Calling cards" in line 19 refer to
    (A) letters of recommendation
    (B) representative topics
    (C) sources of entertainment
    (D) means of identification
    (E) books

Approach: For all word identifications and meanings of words used figuratively, read the passage carefully and decide how the word fits the meaning of the sentence *and* the passage in which it is found. The context of the word "reams" in question 1 suggests that Poe wrote a lot about others of his time, and so choices (D) and (E) can be eliminated. When we substitute the remaining phrases in the sentence, choice (A) is incorrect, because it is awkward and does not fit the sense of the sentence, and choice (C) appears redundant, and so it is also incorrect. The only correct choice is (B), "large amounts."

In question 2, the use of the word "panning" in the passages suggests a negative association, because its context in which Poe was "*panning* some and praising others" is the opposite of "praising." Thus positive associations, such as choice (E), or neutral associations, such as choices (A), (C), and (D), must be incorrect. Only choice (B), "criticizing severely," is correct.

The context of "celluloid corpses," the metaphor to be identified in question 3, is contained in a sentence that describes how Poe's plots were mutilated when made into movies, and so choices (A), (B), (C), and (E) are all incorrect. The only correct choice is (D), "movies."

In question 4, the term "calling cards" suggests choice (D), "means of identification," but a review of the sentences surrounding the term shows that this choice and choice (A) are incorrect. Choice (E) is also incorrect, because the entities described appear in Poe's books, but they are not the books themselves. Choice (C) is also incorrect, because the entities mentioned may be "sources of entertainment" for Poe's readers, but they are for him creations. The only correct answer is choice (B), "representative topics."

Terms That Evaluate Degree and Exclude

You have already worked with questions that ask you to identify the "best" choice and the "most likely" decision. The terms in this section ask for the opposite response. In some cases, questions in the reading passage section ask you to identify a statement with which the author would be *least likely* to agree or the action that the subject of a passage may be *least likely* to undertake. Such questions are the reverse of most questions, and they actually ask you to identify the opposite of the main idea. A second type of question is what might be called "the wrong answer" response—the *except* question. The answer choices for this type of question include four choices with which the author or subject of the passage would agree and one with which the author or subject would not agree. Such a question asks you to identify the one answer that is not included or that does not match the others.

Questions that ask you to identify the "least likely" or "except" answer are usually phrased as follows:

"With which of the following statements would the author (subject) be LEAST likely to agree?"

"In the passage, the author (subject) exhibits all of the following opinions EXCEPT ... ."

Example

1 College information technology administrators have found
2 their servers grinding to a halt as greater numbers have
3 discovered how to enjoy the latest music on the Internet.
4 Students often spend hours listening to music and
5 downloading, while they tie up valuable server time that is
6 supposed to be used for academic pursuits. Rather than to
7 research obscure facts for history or download scientific data
8 for biology, they are searching for the latest CD and
9 downloading their favorite songs. Colleges that have
10 experienced server slowdowns have asked their students to
11 limit the time spent in this pursuit, but their requests have had
12 very little effect. The only way to decrease such time spent
13 online is to place locks on the server, so that it will
14 automatically refuse to connect to the areas that are causing so
15 much difficulty. But, this would be censorship.

(151 words)

1. With which of the following statements would the author be LEAST likely to agree?
   (A) Computers interfere with study time.
   (B) Modern music is a powerful force.
   (C) The Internet is remarkably versatile.
   (D) Colleges should control what students access on the computer.
   (E) College administrators are frustrated.

2. All of the following are mentioned in the passage EXCEPT
   (A) students are downloading music from the Internet
   (B) colleges have experienced server slowdowns
   (C) students are tying up valuable server time
   (D) colleges are limiting student access to music websites
   (E) more time is spent pursuing music than researching academic subjects

Approach: In answering questions of degree and exclusion, you are actually looking for the wrong answer, the choice that is the reverse of the usual reading passage question. Question 1 asks you to identify the statement with which the author would most disagree. When phrased in that manner, choice (D) stands out as the correct choice because of the author's final statement in the passage that signals disagreement with controls. To answer question 2, check each of the answer choices in the passage until you find a choice that is not found in the passage. When you do this, you find that you can locate choices (A), (B), (C), and (E), but not choice (D). The passage only suggests that colleges should do this, but it does not state that they do this, and so choice (D) is the correct answer.

That's it. You have now reviewed all the verbal skills that you must master in order to earn a high score on the SAT verbal section. Now—are you ready to test your skills on the practice tests? Each of the practice tests contains the same items and requirements as the actual SAT verbal sections, so time yourself carefully and stick to the time limits. Put your skills to work!

Chapter 17

Practice Test I

Time: 30 Minutes
30 Questions

For each question in this section, select the best answer among the choices given and darken the appropriate oval on the answer sheet.

Each of the following questions consists of a related main word or phrase pair, followed by five pairs of words or phrases labeled A through E. Select the answer that expresses a relationship that is most similar to the relationship of the main word pair.

EXAMPLE: ORANGE : FRUIT ::

(A) apple : sauce
(B) grape : bunch
(C) red : color
(D) lemon : grapefruit
(E) left : right

1. EVANESCENT : TRANSIENT ::
   (A) new : old
   (B) permanent : fleeting
   (C) profuse : scarce
   (D) obscure : opaque
   (E) generous : penurious

2. FLOWER : FLOURISH ::
   (A) ruffle : rupture
   (B) expedite : stymie
   (C) distend : expand
   (D) ameliorate : relegate
   (E) review : renew

3. FASTIDIOUS : PERFUNCTORY
   (A) meticulous : exacting
   (B) conscientious : scrupulous
   (C) arrogant : egotistical
   (D) rash : wary
   (E) subdued : restrained

4. GARNER : AMASS ::
   (A) efface : impress
   (B) rant : whisper
   (C) placate : enhance
   (D) rescind : abolish
   (E) exhume : resume

5. FACILITATE : EXPEDITE ::
   (A) pulverize : rupture
   (B) compress : distend
   (C) debilitate : weaken
   (D) capitulate : repeat
   (E) mollify : antagonize

6. AMBULATORY : MOBILE ::
   (A) salubrious : nefarious
   (B) fruitful : fertile
   (C) parsimonious : munificent
   (D) luxurious : penurious
   (E) callous : undefiled

7. FLAGRANT : OSTENTATIOUS ::
   (A) reticent : audacious
   (B) vainglorious : unpretentious
   (C) timid : diffident
   (D) pompous : taciturn
   (E) introverted : garrulous

8. ARISTOCRAT : IMPERIOUS ::
   (A) hero : cowardly
   (B) scholar : ignorant
   (C) ballerina : awkward
   (D) peasant : servile
   (E) suppliant : arrogant

9. CIRCUMSPECT : RASH ::
   (A) heedful : prudent
   (B) negligent : lax
   (C) pliant : rigid
   (D) lugubrious : ebullient
   (E) dejected : melancholy

10. CORPUSCLE : BLOOD ::
    (A) red : white
    (B) muscle : tissue
    (C) droplet : water
    (D) body : fluid
    (E) bone : marrow

11. ARTIST : PAINTING ::
    (A) surgeon : body
    (B) poet : paper
    (C) stage : dancer
    (D) writer : story
    (E) sculptor : clay

12. AFFLUENT : WEALTHY ::
    (A) prosperous : generous
    (B) poor : impoverished
    (C) philanthropic : stingy
    (D) antagonistic : palliative
    (E) titillating : inspiring

13. HOST : CONGENIAL ::
    - (A) parsimonious : miser
    - (B) physician : caring
    - (C) coward : valiant
    - (D) connoisseur : knowledgeable
    - (E) director : amiable

14. WHIP : EXCORIATE ::
    - (A) overpower : laurels
    - (B) trophy : punish
    - (C) soothe : emollient
    - (D) light : illuminate
    - (E) mouse : scare

15. BERATE : CALUMNIATE ::
    - (A) incense : appease
    - (B) chide: castigate
    - (C) vilify : praise
    - (D) mollify : nettle
    - (E) tout : deride

16. MULE : RECALCITRANT ::
    - (A) slovenly : pig
    - (B) dullwitted : sheep
    - (C) hyena : intelligent
    - (D) lamb : gentle
    - (E) cow : fierce

17. HOSPITABLE : CORDIAL ::
    - (A) thrifty : frugal
    - (B) contentious : tested
    - (C) cantankerous : tall
    - (D) adamant : indifferent
    - (E) flexible : perverse

18. BIBLIOPHILE : BOOKS ::
    (A) philanthropist : stamps
    (B) etymologist : insects
    (C) lepidopterist : butterflies
    (D) numismatist : cards
    (E) optimist : spectacles

19. INTREPID : VALOROUS ::
    (A) exuberant : prostrate
    (B) insolent : respectful
    (C) ginger : flagrant
    (D) multitudinous : plethoric
    (E) dynamic : static

> The following passage is followed by questions based on its content. Answer the questions that follow *based only on the material that appears in the passage or is suggested by the passage.*

Questions 20–30 are based on the following passage.

1
2   The proliferation of computers in the United States has made a vast change in society in
3   the last decade. Business forecasters who may have once questioned the sanity of technology
4   pioneers that envisioned a computer in every household now claim to have been among the
5   farsighted. Politicians include the aim of making computers available to every schoolchild in
6   their platforms. Schools allocate large amounts of their budgets to obtaining and maintaining
7   computer laboratories, with the goal of making their students technologically viable in a world
8   gone computer-mad. The only people not enjoying the fruits of the revolution are the
9   technophobes, individuals of every age who have not yet been bitten by the computer bug and
10 who express no shame in admitting as much. For them, there is little sympathy and no organized
11 group exists to protect them from the slings and arrows—the abuse and humiliation—cast upon
12 them by their technologically superior acquaintances.
13
14   And, what have they done to merit our abuse? The mind reels when considering their
15 transgressions. While the rest of us are busily checking our e-mail messages three or more times
16 daily, and hitting DELETE to eliminate the multitude of offers appearing among our personal
17 messages that would have been telephone calls in days past, the technophobes are wasting their
18 time meeting with people and engaging in verbal communication. As we seek to save minutes in
19 our business transactions by using the quaintly named "e-commerce" and sit staring at our
20 flickering screens, waiting for the busy and overloaded sites to clear and for the graphics to load

21 (or for the "site not available" message to force us to restart the process), those miscreants are
22 dialing "800" numbers and engaging in pleasant, if time-wasting, conversation with order takers.
23 Some even write out their orders, attach checks, and mail them by what has come to be known
24 among the technologically advanced as "snail mail." Even their personal lives remain untouched
25 by the computer revolution as they maintain the superiority of their primitive mating habits. The
26 technophobes reject the efficiency of "chat rooms," online personals ads, and e-mail courtship,
27 all the while lauding the benefits of personal contact, of meeting people in person and of making
28 "eye contact."

30   Something must be done to educate the technophobes, to raise them from their depths of
31 blissful technological ignorance and to make them a part of the brave new world of computers.
32 Rather than to scorn the technologically challenged of this nation, we have a duty to provide
33 them with the "benefits" that their technologically superior fellow human beings enjoy. Why
34 should they be free to share conversation over cups of coffee instead of having to wait for the
35 hardly instant "instant message" to appear. To laugh in real time at another person's joke rather
36 than to enjoy a solitary laugh while staring at a screen? To purchase items that they have
37 actually—not virtually—seen? We owe them our total support—to do anything less would not
38 be human.

20. According to the passage, "e-commerce" is another word for
    (A) chat rooms
    (B) excellent business opportunities
    (C) instant messages
    (D) business transactions
    (E) everyday commerce

21. A good title for the passage is
    (A) "A Look Into the Future"
    (B) "Computers for Education"
    (C) "A Mission of Mercy"
    (D) "Saving Time Through Technology"
    (E) "The 'Benefits' of Technology"

22. The phrase "computer-mad" in line 8 is used to suggest
    (A) that computers have increased mental disorders.
    (B) that computers are found in every aspect of human life.
    (C) that people are angry at computers.
    (D) that the world is in chaos because of computers.
    (E) nothing at all.

23. The best example of figurative language in the passage is
    (A) computer laboratories (line 7)
    (B) slings and arrows (line 11)
    (C) "e-commerce" (line 19)
    (D) "chat rooms" (line 26)
    (E) "eye contact" (line 28)

24. The author mentions all of the following as being enthusiastic about computers EXCEPT
    (A) politicians
    (B) business forecasters
    (C) schools
    (D) computer programmers
    (E) technology pioneers

25. Based on the second paragraph of the passage, one can infer that
    (A) technophobes are criminals.
    (B) technology saves people time.
    (C) computers make the world run in a more efficient manner.
    (D) human contact is diminished by the use of computers.
    (E) the writer hates computer users.

26. The author uses the phrase "snail mail" in line 24 to mean
    (A) slow computer e-mail
    (B) overseas mail
    (C) facsimile transmission
    (D) air mail
    (E) ground mail

27. The author's tone is best described as
    (A) bitterly sarcastic
    (B) confused
    (C) gently mocking
    (D) serious
    (E) genuinely puzzled

28. Which of the following statements is the author of the passage LEAST likely to agree with?
    (A) In technology, the race belongs to the swiftest.
    (B) In the future, everyone will own a computer.
    (C) Computers have improved everyone's life.
    (D) Not using a computer makes a person completely ineffective today.
    (E) Computers have benefited children.

29. In exhibiting how technophobes are deprived by not using computers, the author cites all of the following EXCEPT
    (A) e-mail
    (B) business transactions
    (C) chat rooms
    (D) online education
    (E) instant messages

30. The phrase "slings and arrows" in the first paragraph is meant to mean
    (A) physical violence against children.
    (B) insults against the technologically superior.
    (C) abuse and humiliation against technophobes.
    (D) broken hearts from online romances gone sour.
    (E) computer operating system failures.

Chapter 18

Practice Test I Answers

Analogies (Questions 1–19)

1. EVANESCENT : TRANSIENT

    Answer (D) is correct. The terms in the main word pair mean approximately the same. Thus, choices (A), (B), (C), and (E) are incorrect, because they represent opposite relationships.

2. FLOWER : FLOURISH

    Answer (C) is correct. The terms in the main word pair name the same action. Choices(A), (D), and (E) are incorrect, because the words in each of these pairs have no necessary relationship. The word pair in choice (B) consists of opposite actions.

3. FASTIDIOUS : PERFUNCTORY

    Answer (D) is correct. The terms in the main word pair are adjectives that name opposite types of behavior or personalities. Thus, choices (A), (B), (C), and (E) are all incorrect, because each word pair contains adjectives that name similar types of behavior or personalities.

4. GARNER : AMASS

    Answer (D) is correct. The terms in the main word pair exhibit a degree relationship. To garner is to gather, but to amass is to garner in a more aggressive manner. Choice (A) is incorrect, because the words in the pair are opposites. Choices (C) and (E) have no necessary relationship. Choice (B) exhibits a strong degree relationship, but the terms are reversed.

5. FACILITATE : EXPEDITE

    Answer (C) is correct. The terms in the main word pair name the same action. Choices (B) and (E) contain opposite relationships, while no relationship exists in (A) and (D).

6. AMBULATORY : MOBILE

    Answer (B) is correct. The terms in the main word pair are adjectives that describe the same capability. Choices (A), (C), (D), and (E) all contain adjective pairs that are opposites.

133

7. FLAGRANT : OSTENTATIOUS

Answer (C) is correct. The terms in the main word pair are adjectives that describe the same quality. Choices (A), (B), and (E) all contain adjective pairs that are opposites, and the terms in choice (D) have no necessary relationship.

8. ARISTOCRAT : IMPERIOUS

Answer (D) is correct. The terms in the main word pair contain a noun and an adjective correctly associated with the noun. Choices (A), (B), (C), and (E) all contain word pairs in which a noun is described by an adjective that is the opposite of the correct description.

9. CIRCUMSPECT : RASH

Answer (D) is correct. The terms in the main word pair contain adjectives that describe opposite qualities. Choices (A), (B), and (E) contain adjectives that describe similar qualities, and no relationship exists in the word pair in choice (C).

10. CORPUSCLE : BLOOD

Answer (C) is correct. The terms in the main word pair are related as the part to the whole. Choices (A) and (B) have no necessary relationship, and the relationships in choices (C) and (E) are weakly connected and reversed.

11. ARTIST : PAINTING

Answer (D) is correct. The relationship in the main word pair is between a profession and the product of that occupation. All the other choices exhibit relationships between a profession and items worked with.

12. AFFLUENT : WEALTHY

Answer (B) is correct. The relationship in the main word pair is between two adjectives that mean the same. All the other choices contain word pairs that are opposite in meaning or that have no relationship.

13. HOST : CONGENIAL

Answer (D) is correct. The relationship in the main word pair is between a noun and an adjective that accurately describes that noun. Choice (A) contains an accurate pair, but the words are reversed. Choice (C) contains an opposite relationship. All the other choices contain word pairs that could but do not necessarily relate.

14. WHIP : EXCORIATE

    Answer (D) is correct. The relationship in the main word pair is between a noun and its expected action. The terms are reversed in choice (C), and none of the other choices contain a necessary relationship.

15. BERATE : CALUMNIATE

    Answer (B) is correct. The relationship in the main word pair is lesser to greater degree. All the other choices contain opposite relationships.

16. MULE : RECALCITRANT

    Answer (D) is correct. The relationship in the main word pair is between a noun and its characteristic. Although choices (A) and (B) represent the correct relationship, the words are reversed. The remaining choices are inaccurate.

17. HOSPITABLE : CORDIAL

    Answer (A) is correct. The relationship in the main word pair is between two adjectives that mean the same. None of the other choices contain this relationship.

18. BIBLIOPHILE : BOOKS

    Answer (C) is correct. The relationship in the main word pair is between a noun and the item that the noun collects or studies. None of the other choices contain correct pairs.

19. INTREPID : VALOROUS

    Answer (D) is correct. The relationship in the main word pair is between two adjectives that have the same meaning. All the other choices contain word pairs that are opposites.

Reading Comprehension (Questions 20–30)

20. Answer (D) is correct. See lines 18–19 ("As we seek to save minutes in our business transactions …."). Although the passage does refer to (A), (B), (C), and (E), they are not linked to the term.

21. Answer (E) is correct. Choice (A) is not correct, because the passage does not project into the future. Choices (B) and (D) are too point specific. The tongue-in-cheek nature of the paragraph might be expressed in (C), but (E) provides more indication of the satire through the use of quotation marks around the word "benefits."
22. Answer (B) is correct. The passage provides no indication of mental disturbance or human anger due to computer use, and so choices (A) and (C) are incorrect. And the inconveniences noted in the passage are not the chaos of choice (D). Something is happening, and so (E) is also incorrect.
23. Answer (B) is correct. The other choices all contain terms that do not represent something other than what they say, but "slings and arrows" figuratively refers to the intellectual abuse that people suffer.
24. Answer (D) is correct. All the other classes of people are mentioned in the passage.
25. Answer (D) is correct. The paragraph emphasizes the use of the computer over face-to-face transactions.
26. Answer (E) is correct. The term "snail mail" refers to the slowness of the mail, like the movement of a snail, and ground mail is the slowest of the five choices.
27. Answer (C) is correct. The author is clear in his objections, and so choices (B) and (E) are incorrect. No attack is launched within the passage, and so choice (A) is incorrect; and the sometimes epic language used to describe saving the technophobes brings enough humor to the piece to make (D) incorrect.
28. Answer (D) is correct. The term "LEAST likely to agree with" should be viewed as meaning "most likely to disagree with." Although the author may disagree with several of the statements, the one that the author would most disagree with is the statement that is disproved in the passage.
29. Answer (D) is correct. All the other items are mentioned in the passage.
30. Answer (C) is correct. In line 11, the passage definnes the term in an appositive.

Chapter 19

Practice Test II

Time: 30 Minutes
30 Questions

For each question in this section, select the best answer among the choices given and darken the appropriate oval on the answer sheet.

Each of the following sentences has one or two blanks, each blank indicating that a word has been omitted. Select the answer that contains the word or word pair that best fits the meaning of the sentence.

EXAMPLE: The voters fear that giving aid to foreign nations will _____ American financial resources.

(A) replete
(B) burgeon
(C) deplete
(D) jettison
(E) impede

1. The CIA agent moved _____ through Eastern Europe during the years that the Communists were in power.

   (A) prodigiously
   (B) surreptitiously
   (C) capriciously
   (D) pusillanimously
   (E) figuratively

2. A lengthy mathematical formula might _____ some people, but those who have studied calculus are easily up to the challenge.

   (A) whet
   (B) spurn
   (C) obscure
   (D) stymie
   (E) placate

137

3. In order to lose weight and to lower cholesterol, a person must be _____ in diet and avoid overeating.
   - (A) listless
   - (B) profuse
   - (C) ambivalent
   - (D) enigmatic
   - (E) abstemious

4. Despite the pleas of the murderer's mother and grandmother, the jury refused to recommend _____ to the judge in sentencing.
   - (A) vibrancy
   - (B) conviviality
   - (C) clemency
   - (D) paucity
   - (E) ascendancy

5. The _____ crimes committed by the defendant made the judge determined to pronounce the harshest sentence allowed by law.
   - (A) irascible
   - (B) hackneyed
   - (C) coherent
   - (D) nefarious
   - (E) alleged

6. The only witness to at first provide the accused with an alibi chose to _____ her testimony when she faced charges of perjury.
   - (A) broadcast
   - (B) recant
   - (C) kindle
   - (D) enhance
   - (E) reject

7. The courts may lessen a sentence for someone who is genuinely sorry, but a _____ defendant will receive the maximum penalty.
   - (A) rescind

(B) premeditated
   (C) recalcitrant
   (D) fraudulent
   (E) novice

8. The _____ of sugar- and fat-filled snack foods in the cabinets _____ the impression that the tenant did not follow a healthy diet.
   (A) affirmation ... indicated
   (B) existence ... contradicted
   (C) paucity ... strengthened
   (D) profusion ... conveyed
   (E) absence ... supported

9. The war hero was _____ in his _____ to rescue American prisoners of war who may have been left in Vietnam when the war ended.
   (A) salubrious ... failure
   (B) dauntless ... refusal
   (C) antediluvian ... effort
   (D) tenacious ... quest
   (E) hackneyed ... plan

10. The manufacturer used her _____ wealth to provide numerous shelters and job training for _____ of domestic abuse.
    (A) questionable ... observers
    (B) vast ... perpetrators
    (C) plentiful ... objects
    (D) prodigious ... victims
    (E) anonymous ... reporters

11. Most personal injury defense lawyers seem to believe that a cash _____ of any size will easily _____ most victims.
    (A) rebate ... quiet
    (B) settlement ... placate

(C) discrepancy ... revive
(D) transaction ... satisfy
(E) receipt ... mollify

12. The band director _____ regular practice sessions in order to produce the most _____ and skillfully played music possible.
    (A) avoids ... innocuous
    (B) attends ... spontaneous
    (C) cancels ... inept
    (D) schedules ... cacophonous
    (E) requires ... euphonious

13. I refused to _____ to her demands that I work late for no extra pay, despite her continued requests.
    (A) blunder
    (B) acquiesce
    (C) levitate
    (D) facilitate
    (E) celebrate

14. She used _____ to trick all of us into giving up our company pensions to invest in a worthless underwater island.
    (A) effervescence
    (B) hilarity
    (C) reserve
    (D) guile
    (E) bribery

15. The patient surprised his doctors by becoming _____ and walking on his own soon after his knee surgery.
    (A) ambivalent
    (B) fallow
    (C) ambulatory
    (D) listless
    (E) lugubrious

The following passages are followed by questions based on their content. Answer the questions that follow *based only on the material that appears in the passages or is suggested by the passages*.

Questions 16–30 are based on the following passages.

PASSAGE ONE

1 The issue of censorship has become even
2 more complicated than in the past when we
3 worried only about whether our children
4 were attending "proper" movies and reading
5 decent books. Television often brings
6 unsuitable material right into our homes, the
7 computer draws inappropriate images from
8 the internet, and billboards scream sex at us
9 as we drive down the highway or stand
10 waiting for our bus or subway car to take us
11 to our destinations. A movie that is rated
12 PG-13 leads the unsuspecting parent to
13 believe that it is suitable for the young teen
14 to view. Once ensconced in the padded
15 theater seat, the unsuspecting parent finds
16 that the language or sexual situations
17 included in the film for laughs actually
18 cause an adult to cringe while sitting next
19 to the "child" that the rating was created to
20 protect.
21   Who can set the standard as to what is
22 "obscene" and, therefore, unacceptable? In
23 1970, members of the committee that
24 produced the Report of the United States
25 President's Commission on Obscenity
26 struggled and failed to define what was
27 obscene and pornographic. More than a
28 decade later, in 1986, the United States
29 Attorney General's Council on Pornography
30 (often called the Meese Commission) was
31 no more effective. Their findings were as
32 inconclusive as those of the 1970 report.
33 What that means is that we are left to police
34 our children ourselves. No one else can
35 decide for the individual what is offensive or
36 not. And, maybe that is best.
37
38
PASSAGE TWO
40
41   Censorship is a very clear issue and a
42 very important one to a society that must
43 protect its most vulnerable members from
44 assault by images that offend. Anti-
45 censorship proponents are fond of hiding
46 behind First Amendment rights whenever
47 called upon to defend their claims that all
48 media should be free to publish and
49 broadcast whatever they may wish. What
50 they fail to consider is how the Founding
51 Fathers would react if they were to be
52 confronted with the type of material that
53 their amendments are today called upon to
54 defend. The speech to which the First
55 Amendment granted freedom was a far cry
56 from the language and images that shoot
57 across television and movies screens, that
58 pepper magazines and billboards, and that
59 sneak their way into Internet searches.
60   Despite the claims of many censorship
61 opponents that no one can establish a
62 standard of what constitutes unacceptable
63 material, a means of establishing a standard
64 **can** be achieved. Language is standardized,
65 via the use of grammar and vocabulary, so
66 that each language with a written tradition

141

67 can determine what is standard or non-
68 standard language. The same may also be
69 possible in establishing what is acceptable
70 language or an acceptable image. Standards
71 in many areas are developed based on the
72 beliefs and views of the majority of a
73 society. How else might we maintain
74 structure and order—and hold the forces of
75 anarchy at bay?

16. The author of Passage One mentions all of the following as contemporary sites of potentially unsuitable material EXCEPT
    (A) movies
    (B) television
    (C) billboards
    (D) books
    (E) computer

17. According to Passage One, the word "proper" in line 4 is used to mean the same as
    (A) mannerly
    (B) new
    (C) accurate
    (D) decent
    (E) adventure

18. The author in Passage One places the word "child" within quotation marks in line 19 because
    (A) someone aged 13 is not really a child.
    (B) the parent is very old.
    (C) no one likes being called a child.
    (D) the parent feels less comfortable than the child with movie content.
    (E) no reason.

19. Based on the first paragraph of Passage One, one can infer that
    (A) the writer feels helpless
    (B) the writer feels that the issue of censorship is unimportant
    (C) the writer feels that the issue of censorship is complicated
    (D) the writer is a neutral observer
    (E) the writer is a movie enthusiast

20. The author's tone in Passage One is best described as
    (A) capricious
    (B) argumentative
    (C) sarcastic
    (D) thoughtful
    (E) ironic

21. The term "anti-censorship proponents" that appears in lines 44–45 of Passage Two is used to mean
    (A) pornographers
    (B) the Founding Fathers
    (C) those who favor censorship
    (D) censorship opponents
    (E) government figures

22. The author of Passage Two mentions all of the following as contemporary sites of potentially unsuitable language and images EXCEPT
    (A) magazines
    (B) television
    (C) billboards
    (D) Internet
    (E) radio

23. According to Passage Two, grammar and vocabulary have been used to do which of the following?
    (A) stop censorship
    (B) teach people to write
    (C) standardize censorship
    (D) standardize language
    (E) create anarchy

24. With which of the following statements is the author of Passage Two LEAST likely to agree?
    (A) The rights of children are more important than those of adults.
    (B) Censorship should not be allowed in a free society.

(C) The rights of the few should take precedence over the rights of the many.

(D) The rights of the many should take precedence over the rights of the few.

(E) No one should have any rights.

25. The author of Passage Two infers that "the forces of anarchy" are held at bay by which of the following?
    (A) language standards
    (B) grammar
    (C) vocabulary
    (D) social standards
    (E) threats of force

26. The passage differ in that
    (A) the author of Passage Two expresses an opinion but the author of Passage One does not.
    (B) Passage One is more humorous.
    (C) the author of Passage One expresses an opinion but the author of Passage Two does not.
    (D) only Passage One uses facts to support the opinions.
    (E) Passage Two was written more recently.

27. The authors of both passages would most likely agree with which of the following statements?
    (A) No one can decide for the individual what is offensive.
    (B) Society does not need further controls.
    (C) Children must be protected from inappropriate language and images.
    (D) The government sets moral standards.
    (E) Parents should not have powers.

28. The term "Founding Fathers" in lines 50–51 of Passage Two refers to
    (A) originators of the censorship movement
    (B) movie and publishing pioneers
    (C) writers of the First Amendment

(D) originators of the anti-censorship movement
(E) the early wilderness explorers

29. Which is more likely to be surprising to the respective author?
    (A) Passage One author: a clear definition of "obscene"
    (B) Passage Two author: a standard for censorship
    (C) Passage Two author: sexual situations in movies
    (D) Passage Two author: anti-censorship proponents
    (E) Passage One author: unsuitable material entering homes via television

30. Which of the following is the most appropriate title for Passage Two?
    (A) "No Censorship, No Way"
    (B) "A Time for Compromise"
    (C) "A Standard Is Needed"
    (D) "Understanding the First Amendment"
    (E) "Freedom for All"

Chapter 20

Practice Test II Answers

Sentence Completions (Questions 1–15)

1. Answer (B) is correct. The context is established by the condition that the Communists were in power at the time.

2. Answer (D) is correct. The conjunction "but" creates opposition between two parts of the sentence, and so the missing words must provide the opposite effect of being "up to the challenge."

3. Answer (E) is correct. The context of losing weight requires that limitations in diet exist, and so a related word is required. The remaining choices have no relationship to restrictions.

4. Answer (C) is correct. The word "despite" creates opposition in the sentence between the pleas and the jury's expected recommendations.

5. Answer (D) is correct. The judge's pronouncement of the "harshest sentence" points to particularly evil, or "nefarious," crimes rather than the other relatively tame adjectives.

6. Answer (B) is correct. The negative possibility of a charge of perjury sets the context in the sentence.

7. Answer (C) is correct. The conjunction "but" creates opposition between the sentence for "someone who is genuinely sorry" and the described defendant.

8. Answer (D) is correct. When the first word of each of the pairs is tried, choices (B) and (D) are both possibilities, but substituting the second word of the pair affirms the choice as (D).

9. Answer (D) is correct. When the first word of each of the pairs is tried, the positive connotations of choices (A), (B), and (D) all seem to be possibilities. Substituting the second word of the pair eliminates all but (D).

10. Answer (D) is correct. The sentence context calls for substantial wealth to aid those who have suffered abuse. Choice (B) seemed like a possibility, because the first word was perfect, but good sense dictates that a shelter should not be provided for the "perpetrators" of abuse.

11. Answer (B) is correct. The context of the sentence is legal, with its mention of "personal injury defense lawyers," and so the word "settlement" rather than any other relating to money is in order.
12. Answer (E) is correct. The clue in this sentence lies in matching the second word of the pair by finding a word that matches "skillfully played music." Although (B) may seem to be a possibility, just having the band director attend regular practice sessions would not result in positive outcomes, and so this is incorrect. Aside from (E), the other choices do not relate to positive music outcomes.
13. Answer (B) is correct. None of the other choices provide the possible meaning of "give in."
14. Answer (D) is correct. The context clue in this sentence is "trick," which points to the use of "guile."
15. Answer (C) is correct. A definition of the term needed is found in the sentence, in the phrase that follows the conjunction "and."

Readng Comprehension (Questions 16–30)

16. Answer (D) is correct. The reference to books is not mentioned as a contemporary site but in lines 4–5 as a past source of concern.
17. Answer (D) is correct. The description of the movies is connected by "and" to the description of "decent" books.
18. Answer (D) is correct. The other choices are opinions, but the parent's discomfort is stated in lines 18–19 of the passage.
19. Answer (C) is correct. The writer states that the issue is "even more complicated."
20. Answer (D) is correct. The remaining choices all require turns of phrase and shows of emotional, slanted language, which do not appear in the passage.
21. Answer (D) is correct. Taken in parts, the term means "those in favor of being against censorship."
22. Answer (E) is correct. All the other choices are mentioned in the first paragraph of the passage.
23. Answer (D) is correct. The author states in lines 64–65 that language is standardized through grammar and vocabulary.

24. Answer (C) is correct. In the final lines of the second paragraph of the passage, the author speaks of the standards developed "based on the beliefs and views of the majority of a society."
25. Answer (D) is correct. No "threats of force" appear in the passage, and so choice (E) is incorrect, and the other three choices are connected.
26. Answer (D) is correct. Both passages express opinions, making (A) and (C) incorrect, and neither is humorous (B). No one can tell when either passage was written, making (E) incorrect. Passage One supplies facts about the two commissions, while Passage Two presents only unsupported opinion.
27. Answer (C) is correct. The different stances of the authors expressed in (A), (B), (D), and (E) are incorrect. Both authors do care about protecting children, but via different means.
28. Answer (C) is correct. The passage connects them with "their amendments" in lines 53–55.
29. Answer (A) is correct. All the other situations are indicated as present or happening.
30. Answer (C) is correct. The author calls for the setting of a standard in lines 60–64.

Chapter 21

Practice Test III

Time: 30 Minutes
30 Questions

For each question in this section, select the best answer among the choices given and darken the appropriate oval on the answer sheet.

Each of the following sentences has one or two blanks, each blank indicating that a word has been omitted. Select the answer that contains the word or word pair that best fits the meaning of the sentence.

EXAMPLE: The voters fear that giving aid to foreign nations will _____ American financial resources.

(A) replete
(B) burgeon
(C) deplete
(D) jettison
(E) impede

---

1. Leonardo DaVinci's painting of mysterious Mona Lisa is said to portray her with a(n) _____ smile on her face.

    (A) fraudulent
    (B) listless
    (C) effervescent
    (D) enigmatic
    (E) foolish

2. A university library should contain a _____ of books, in order to provide properly for the research needs of students.

    (A) summary
    (B) vilification
    (C) myriad
    (D) paucity
    (E) number

3. The _____ prosecutor refused to allow the lack of evidence to prevent her from going to trial.
   (A) humane
   (B) tenacious
   (C) salubrious
   (D) erudite
   (E) malevolent

4. Once-famous rock star Oliver had huge record sales with "Jean," then faded into _____.
   (A) opacity
   (B) discrepancy
   (C) parsimony
   (D) reality
   (E) obscurity

5. The secret to living well among the rich and famous is to have _____ amounts of money and time to _____.
   (A) meager ... work
   (B) unlimited ... panhandle
   (C) specific ... exist
   (D) copious ...socialize
   (E) unknown ... read

6. The _____ of the normally mild-mannered candidate's _____ attack on his opponent's character shocked the press.
   (A) mildness ...vicious
   (B) maliciousness ... friendly
   (C) virulence ... vitriolic
   (D) charm ...pleasant
   (E) novelty ... old

7. A student who takes his 80-year-old aunt to his high school senior prom should expect that his classmates will view her as _____.
   (A) youthful

- (B) antediluvian
- (C) fashionable
- (D) zany
- (E) bizarre

8. Sending troops into battle without concern for their safety makes soldiers feel as if they are _____.
   - (A) hypocritical
   - (B) valuable
   - (C) viable
   - (D) expendable
   - (E) ephemeral

9. In order to _____ the shipment, the company will fill out the paperwork in advance and send a truck to meet the plane.
   - (A) contaminate
   - (B) anticipate
   - (C) mitigate
   - (D) dispute
   - (E) expedite

10. Too many _____ voters fail to _____ their right to vote in local and national elections.
    - (A) hopeful ...request
    - (B) registered ... exercise
    - (C) new ... give up
    - (D) silly ...claim
    - (E) unregistered ...claim

11. According to the doctor's _____, the patient will have to undergo surgery to correct the problem.
    - (A) diagnosis
    - (B) precepts
    - (C) cranium
    - (D) prognosis
    - (E) pantheon

12. The three groups formed a _____ to jointly lobby Congress to supply aid for the program.
    (A) friendship
    (B) congregation
    (C) prescription
    (D) coalition
    (E) antagonism

Each of the following questions consists of a related main word or phrase pair, followed by five pairs of words or phrases labeled A through E. Select the answer that expresses a relationship that is most similar to the relationship of the main word pair.

EXAMPLE: ORANGE : FRUIT ::

(A) apple : sauce
(B) grape : bunch
(C) red : color
(D) lemon : grapefruit
(E) left : right

---

13. DOCTOR : PATIENT ::
    (A) student : principal
    (B) actor : director
    (C) attorney : client
    (D) judge : jury
    (E) editor : reporter

14. FRAUDULENT : AUTHENTIC ::
    (A) pleasant : agreeable
    (B) arrogant : proud
    (C) excellent : superior
    (D) deliberate : accidental
    (E) deceptive : false

15. REPRIMAND : DENOUNCE ::
    (A) summon : subpoena
    (B) alarm : warn
    (C) compete : rival

- (D) foretell : soothsayer
- (E) perform : actor

16. KITTEN : MEOWS ::
    - (A) barks : puppy
    - (B) donkey : brays
    - (C) bird : flies
    - (D) crows : rooster
    - (E) turkey : whinnies

17. CIRCUMFERENCE : CIRCLE ::
    - (A) altitude : triangle
    - (B) axis : graph
    - (C) diagonal : rectangle
    - (D) equator : earth
    - (E) hemisphere : globe

18. MILLIONAIRE : BILLIONAIRE ::
    - (A) inch : yard
    - (B) liter : kiloliter
    - (C) foot : mile
    - (D) meter : millimeter
    - (E) half : whole

19. ANALGESIC : PAIN ::
    - (A) ice : cold
    - (B) poison : antidote
    - (C) soporific : sleep
    - (D) antacid : indigestion
    - (E) salve : bandage

20. GIGGLE : LAUGH ::
    - (A) speak : talk
    - (B) run : drive
    - (C) walk : sit
    - (D) stand : turn
    - (E) whisper : shout

21. HAZARD : GOLF ::
    (A) goalpost : football
    (B) ice : hockey
    (C) hurdle : track
    (D) bat : baseball
    (E) hoop : basketball

22. ENIGMATIC : INSCRUTABLE ::
    (A) surreptitious : covert
    (B) simultaneous : sporadic
    (C) convivial : reticent
    (D) aromatic : odoriferous
    (E) true : unreal

The following passage is followed by questions based on its content. Answer the questions that follow *based only on the material that appears in the passage or is suggested by the passage.*

Questions 23–30 are based on the following passage.

The art of magazine article writing becomes more craft and less creative artistry as the years wear on. Rather than seize the inspiration and go with an idea, the too-experienced writer usually finds that the ideas are created, the inspiration manufactured, and the artistry tempered by attention to editorial guidelines, word count, and audience anticipation. In short, writing becomes rote, pulsing word rhythms become pap, and ingenious turns of phrase become trite.

What emerges, then, is a document that resembles nothing so much as what Hamlet replied to Polonius when asked what he was reading, "Words, words, words." Sometimes our timing is perfect and we play words against each other so skillfully that even our worst critics, we writers, of course, grudgingly admit to success. At other times, the ideas seem forced and our management of them inept, even horrifying when compared with what could have been written, what we might have written if what—if we had the time? If we had the material? If we had the desire? That last is, perhaps, most disturbing of all to writers who feel that they have lost IT, whatever IT may have been. Sometimes IT simply means inspiration, a new way of looking at old ideas and circumstances. When that happens, a writer has two choices —neither pleasant—either close up shop and move to another location/profession or recharge the creative battery.

Bringing a new perspective to writing can be as easy as taking time away from writing to deadlines and to simply observe the world surrounding. Once away from what has to be written—a sort of canned creativity—many writers find they can recapture some of the freshness that they have lost in viewing the world surrounding. Still others need new places and new people to excite their senses. They must transplant themselves into less familiar, more exotic locales that require them to deal in a different way with their everyday concerns. For some, the fire has gone out and no amount of stoking will rekindle it. For them, writing has become a business— and no longer a profitable business nor even one that permits a living. Among this sad group, a career change or modification is in order. The time may have come to move from the exciting, if somewhat precarious, world of freelance writing to taking a staff position somewhere, anywhere, that will allow them to write.

If that does not work, then the onetime freelancer may just have to accept the fact that, whatever he or she once had, IT is no more. The fantasy for some at this point is to think of becoming an editor, to take out one's blue pencil and to brutalize someone else's work. Most writers tend to think that editing is something that anyone can do, but, of course, it is not. Too often, writers at this stage of their careers choose not to recall the statement made by Robert Giroux in *The Education of an Editor* (1982): "Most editors are failed writers—but so are most writers."

23. According to the passage, IT refers to which of the following?
    (A) personal attractiveness
    (B) acclaim
    (C) professional recognition
    (D) inspiration
    (E) religion

24. In lines 51–52, the metaphor of a fire is used to refer to which of the following?
    (A) the aging writer
    (B) the magazine editors
    (C) the creative spirit
    (D) the writer's talent
    (E) none of the above

25. According to the passage, which of the following is the writer's worst critic?
    (A) the editors
    (B) the public
    (C) family members
    (D) writers themselves
    (E) Robert Giroux

26. The following title best suggests the main idea of the passage:
    (A) "The Writer's Life"
    (B) "Making Writing Meaningful"
    (C) "Becoming an Editor"
    (D) "Recapturing Creativity in Writing"
    (E) "Having IT"

27. The author of this passage would be least likely to agree with which of the following statements?
    (A) Writing is a real profession.
    (B) Writers can recapture inspiration.
    (C) Writers and editors are similar.
    (D) Sometimes writing becomes stale.
    (E) Writing should follow a formula.

28. In this passage, the author's reference to the "blue pencil" in lines 67–69 refers to
    (A) gratuitous vandalism
    (B) random coloring
    (C) the editing process
    (D) the pencil used for rejections
    (E) none of the above

29. The words in lines 24 and 25 are underlined
    (A) because they are foreign terms
    (B) to make them stand out
    (C) to emphasize writers' fears
    (D) to link them to editors
    (E) in error

30. According the passage, the writer in need of creative recharging must
    (A) travel abroad
    (B) stay home and meditate
    (C) go to a tropical island
    (D) simply take time off
    (E) exercise

# Chapter 22

Practice Test III Answers

Sentence Completions (Questions 1–12)

1. Answer (D) is correct. The context is established by the clue word "mysterious" that eliminates the possibility of the other answer choices, which have no connection to the context.

2. Answer (C) is correct. The context is established by the words "university" and "research needs," and the conjunction "in order to" suggests a cause-and-effect relationship.

3. Answer (B) is correct. The context is established by the words "refused" and "to prevent her" that show the strength of the prosecutor's convictions.

4. Answer (E) is correct. The context is established by the adjective phrase "Once-famous" and the verb "faded," to exhibit the loss of recognition.

5. Answer (D) is correct. The context is set by the terms "living well" and "rich and famous," which suggest that a large amount of money is needed. When the first word of each answer pair is tried, choices (B) and (D) seem possible, but substitution of the second word of the two pairs makes the choice clearly (D).

6. Answer (C) is correct. The context is established by the terms "normally" and "shocked," because they imply that the candidate acted in a way that was the opposite of his usual behavior. When the first word of each answer pair is tried, choices (B) and (C) seem possible, but substituting the second word of the pairs makes the choice clearly (C).

7. Answer (B) is correct. The context is established by the "80-year-old aunt" whose appearance would be "antediluvian" to high school seniors.

8. Answer (D) is correct. The context is established by the phrase "without concern for their safety," which suggests that no value is placed on their lives.
9. Answer (E) is correct. The context is established by work completed "in advance" and suggests a desire to move the process forward quickly.
10. Answer (B) is correct. The context is established by the word "right." When the first word of each pair is tried, choices (B) and (E) seem possible, but trying the second word of the pairs determines that the only choice that makes sense is (B).
11. Answer (D) is correct. The context is established by the words "doctor's," "patient," and "undergo surgery." The choice may seem to be between (A) diagnosis and (D) prognosis, but a "diagnosis" identifies the nature illness while the "prognosis" predicts.
12. Answer (D) is correct. The context is established by the terms "groups formed" and "jointly lobby." The term "congregation," (B), means a group, but the purpose to lobby belongs to a "coalition."

Analogies (Questions 13–22)

13. DOCTOR : PATIENT

    Answer (C) is correct. The relationship is between the person's occupation and the term for the person helped. The terms in choice (A) are reversed, and the relationships in (B), (D), and (E) are nearly parallel and, thus, incorrect.

14. FRAUDULENT : AUTHENTIC

    Answer (D) is correct. The relationship is between words that are opposite in meaning, and all the words in the remaining answer choices are similar in meaning.

15. REPRIMAND : DENOUNCE

    Answer (B) is correct. The relationship is between a noun and the verb describing an appropriate action. Choices (A), (C), (D), and (E) all contain the same relationship, but the words are reversed.

16. KITTEN : MEOWS

    Answer (B) is correct. The relationship is between an animal and an appropriate action. Choices (A), (C), and (D) all contain the correct relationship, but the words in the pairs are reversed. Choice (E) is completely incorrect because a turkey does not "whinny."

17. CIRCUMFERENCE : CIRCLE

    Answer (D) is correct. The relationship is between the outside measure of an object and the object. All the remaining choices reflect inside measure or portions of an object.

18. MILLIONAIRE : BILLIONAIRE

    Answer (B) is correct. A millionaire is one-thousandth as wealthy as a billionaire, and only (B) relates the correct proportion in the correct order. Choice (D) contains the same proportion, but the terms are reversed.

19. ANALGESIC : PAIN

    Answer (D) is correct. The relationship is between a medication and the condition it is meant to alleviate. The remaining choices are related but not in the same manner.

20. GIGGLE : LAUGH

    Answer (E) is correct. The relationship is one of degree, because a giggle is a less intense form of a laugh. Choice (A) offers synonyms, and the remaining choices simply pair different actions.

21. HAZARD : GOLF

    Answer (C) is correct. The relationship is between a sport and a physical obstacle that appears in the sport. The remaining choices are composed of either related objects or the sport and a related object, not an obstacle.

22. ENGIMATIC : INSCRUTABLE

    Answer (A) is correct. The relationship is between two adjectives that mean the same. The remaining choices are either unrelated or opposite relationships.

Reading Comprehension (Questions 23–30)

23. Answer (D) is correct. See line 30, which states the definition.
24. Answer (C) is correct. The third paragraph discusses the way in which creativity wanes and suggests efforts to revive it.
25. Answer (D) is correct. See line 20, which presents the connection.
26. Answer (D) is correct. The major part of the passage discusses the loss of inspiration and suggests means to revive creativity. The remaining titles are either too broad or too specific.

27. Answer (E) is correct. The focus of the passage is on recapturing creativity, and so suggesting a formula would be anathema to the author of the passage.
28. Answer (C) is correct. The definition is located in lines 67–69.
29. Answer (C) is correct. The terms are in English, and they identify fears of writers.
30. Answer (D) is correct. See lines 38–41.

Index

Allusions, 22–23
Analogies, 39–82
  approach analogy questions, 40–50
  classification and characteristics, 63–82
    gender classification, 68–69
    group classification, 68–69
    parent-offspring classification, 68–69
    people and professions, 77–82
      and places, 80–82
      and purposes, 79–80
      and qualities, 77–79
    relating objects and ideas, 63–68
      to actions, 67–68
      to special qualities and conditions, 63–65
  general to specific, 71–76
    container to something contained within, 73–75
    general term to specific term, 75–76
    whole to part, 71–73
  size and degree, 57–61
    degree of intensity, 60–61
    relating size, 57–58
    units of measure, 58–60
  troubleshooting, 51–55
    parts of speech, 52–53
    word meanings, 53–55

Completing the sentence, 7–38
Completing word pairs, 9–10
Connotation, 17
Context, 7–15

Denotation, 17

Finding familiar words, 23–24
Finding words that associate, 20–21
Foreign words in sentence completions, 25–29
  sources, 27–29
  types, 25–27
Function words, 14–15

Homographs, 36–38
Homonyms, 32–36
Homophones, 32–36

Identifying word sequence, 13–14
Imposter words, 32
Inference questions, 104–105

People and professions, 77–82

Reading comprehension, 83–124
  author's role questions, 111–118
    attitude, 114–116
    evaluating diction, 119–124
    purpose, 112–114
    tone, 116–118
  drawing inferences, 101–110
    inference questions, 104–105
    paraphrase and interpretation questions, 106–110
    strategies and main ideas, 83–92, 101–103

Reading comprehension, strategies and main ideas (*Cont.*)
    determining main idea, 88–90
    developing strategies, 83–84
    paired passages, 90–91
    reading and understanding the questions, 84–86
    reading the passages effectively, 87
    single passages, 90–91
  text details, 93–99
    finding combined details, 97–99
    trigger words, 93–97

Sentence completion, 7–38
  comparing, 11
  contrasting, 11–13
  explaining directly, 10–11
  finding familiar words, 23–24
  finding words that associate, 20–21
  foreign words, 25–29
  general strategies, 8
  identifying word sequence, 13–14
  imposter words, 32
  one-word blanks, 8, 10, 12, 13
  separating connotation from denotation, 17–19
  separating synonyms, 19–20
  speaking figuratively, 21–22
  two-word blanks, 9, 12, 13
  using allusions, 22–23
  using function words, 14–15
  using the whole sentence, 8–9

Vocabulary building, 1–5

Words that associate, 20–21